Undefeated

Overcoming Prejudice with Grace and Courage

Stephen H. Provost

All material © 2013, 2018, 2020, 2024 Stephen H. Provost

Previously published under the name Stifyn Emrys.

Cover artwork: Public domain images
Cover concept and design: Stephen H. Provost
All interior images are in the public domain.

No part of this book may be reproduced, or stored in a retrieval system, or transmitted in any form or by any means, electronic, mechanical, photocopying, recording, or otherwise, without the express written permission of the publisher.

The contents of this volume and all other works by Stephen H. Provost are entirely the work of the author, with the exception of direct quotations, attributed material used with permission, and items in the public domain. No artificial intelligence ("AI") programs were used to generate content in the creation of this work. No portion of this book, or any of the author's works, may be used to train or provide content for artificial intelligence (AI) programs.

Dragon Crown Books 2024
All rights reserved.

ISBN: 978-1-949971-12-5

To everyone who has ever been bullied,
and to all those who have stood up in their behalf.

Also by the author

Works of Fiction
Crimson Scourge
The Memortality Saga
    Memortality
    Paralucidity
Academy of the Lost Labyrinth
    The Talismans of Time
    Pathfinder of Destiny
The Only Dragon
Identity Break
Nightmare's Eve
Christmas Nightmare's Eve
Feathercap

Works of Nonfiction
A Whole Different League
The Great American Shopping Experience
California's Historic Highways series
    Highway 99
    Highway 101
Highways of the West series
    America's Loneliest Road
    Victory Road
    Sierra Highway
    Lincoln Highway in California (with Gary Kinst)
America's Historic Highways series
    America's First Highways
    Yesterday's Highways

    Highways of the South
Roadside Illustrated series
    Happy Motoring!
    Signpost Up Ahead: The East
    Signpost Up Ahead: The West
Mark Twain's Nevada
The Century Cities series
    Cambria Century, Carson City Century
    Charleston Century, Danville Century
    Fresno Century, Goldfield Century
    Greensboro Century, Huntington Century
    Roanoke Century, San Luis Obispo Century
Fresno Growing Up
Martinsville Memories
The Legend of Molly Bolin
50 Undefeated
The Phoenix Chronicles
    The Osiris Testament
    The Way of the Phoenix
    The Gospel of the Phoenix
The Phoenix Principle
    Forged in Ancient Fires
    Messiah in the Making

Praise for other works

"The complex idea of mixing morality and mortality is a fresh twist on the human condition. ... **Memortality** is one of those books that will incite more questions than it answers. And for fandom, that's a good thing."

— Ricky L. Brown, Amazing Stories

"Punchy and fast paced, **Memortality** reads like a graphic novel. ... (Provost's) style makes the trippy landscapes and mind-bending plot points more believable and adds a thrilling edge to this vivid crossover fantasy."

— Foreword Reviews

"Whether a troubled family's curse or the nightmarish hell created by a new kind of A.I., the autopsy of a vampire or Santa's darker side ... Provost's sure hand guides you down gloomy avenues you do not expect."

— Mark Onspaugh, author of The Faceless One and Deadlight Jack, on **Nightmare's Eve**

"**Memortality** by Stephen Provost is a highly original, thrilling novel unlike anything else out there."

— David McAfee, bestselling author of 33 A.D., 61 A.D., and 79 A.D.

"Profusely illustrated throughout, **Highway 99** is unreservedly recommended as an essential and core addition to every community and academic library's California History collections."

— California Bookwatch

"As informed and informative as it is entertaining and absorbing, **Fresno Growing Up** is very highly recommended for personal, community, and academic library 20th Century American History collections."

— John Burroughs, Reviewer's Bookwatch

STEPHEN H. PROVOST

Preface to the 2024 edition

In 2020, thousands of people are marching through the streets across the United States, protesting the death of a black man named George Floyd — a man who perished while pleading for his life as a Minneapolis police officer knelt on his neck.

A famous civil rights anthem declares that "we overcome someday." Floyd's death and the protests that followed serve as a reminder that "someday" has not yet arrived. But those protests also give us hope that the fight is not lost — that we are still very much in the process of overcoming.

It is in the spirit of this hope that I decided to update and re-release my book *Undefeated*, which profiles individuals from all walks of life and backgrounds who have overcome prejudice, bullying, and oppression. It's been seven years since that work was first published, so I decided to expand the text with five new profiles, bringing the total to a round number: 50. Hence the new title: *50 Undefeated*.

As the tragic, senseless death of George Floyd demonstrates, not victims of bigotry and violence overcome the cruelty visited upon them. Sometimes, the process of overcoming is left to those who come after them, for whom their struggle is a beacon that shines a light on the terror they confronted and, at the same time, shows us the way forward, toward a new hope and a better world.

Those who have persevered give us reason to nurture that hope. Their examples show us what great things are possible when the best of the human spirit rises up and shouts, "No more!" to those with the worst of intentions. Such people are profiled in this work.

50 UNDEFEATED

They've endured abuse, false accusation, and imprisonment. They've overcome depression, substance abuse, and physical limitations.

They've been ridiculed and marginalized because they're "different," but they've made those differences their strength. Intersex Belgian model Halle Gaby Odiele (one of the five new people I've chosen to profile) realized: "I didn't have to follow the norm, because I wasn't the norm."

And they've helped others rise up in hope in the face of cruel, even tragic injustice.

The video of George Floyd gasping for breath as he lay pinned face-down in the street by a police officer awakened many to the stark reality of police violence against people of color. Many of us had ignored it in the past; some of us had not even wanted to acknowledge that it existed.

George Floyd revealed the awful truth of it as he died, in images so clear we could no longer turn away.

His longtime friend Stephen Jackson, who's also profiled in these pages, vowed that his name would become a clarion call for change. And Floyd's 6-year-old daughter rode on Jackson's shoulders, smiling as she declared, "Daddy changed the world!" Like others profiled here, Jackson isn't perfect. But he represents the determination to overcome the odds and fight for what he believes in; hence his inclusion here. In addition to Jackson, new entries in *50 Undefeated* are Katherine Johnson, Marcie Free, Hanne Gaby Odiele, and Lou Ferrigno. I've also added Mark Twain to the mix. (You can find out more about him in my book *Mark Twain's Nevada*.)

The courageous people profiled in these pages are proof that we can. The horrors they endured are proof that we must. The idea for this book came to me, as such ideas often do, first thing in the morning when I was just waking up out of a sound sleep. But the inspiration — or rather the inspirations — behind it can be traced back many years.

Undefeated was, incidentally, my father's favorite early work of mine. I'm proud to present this updated version.

Introduction

When I was a child, I was not the most popular kid in school. Not by a long shot. I had the advantage of being a white male, but it seems I was a little *too* white. This was back in the 1970s, and kids growing up in Southern California, about 15 miles from the beach, were expected to get a tan. It was a mark of achievement to some extent. Unfortunately, the Danish genes I inherited from my mother's side overpowered my father's French DNA, and I couldn't seem to muster that bronzed "surfer dude" look if my life depended on it. And sometimes, it felt like it did.

To make matters worse, I developed a love of popcorn (smothered in butter, of course) and a sedentary lifestyle that pushed the needle on that pesky scale about 30 pounds past where it should have been. I was a bit of an introvert already, so it wasn't long before I became a target of my classmates' pubescent derision. The Great White Whale, they called me.

I withdrew further, became even more introverted, and started spending more time off to myself reading books and watching professional sports. Because I looked at myself as an underdog, I got in the habit of rooting for teams that were underdogs (unless, of course, they were playing against my hometown team).

When I wasn't reading or watching Monday Night Football, I'd crank up the stereo and start listening to my favorite tunes. KISS was my band of choice, larger-than-life heroes in painted faces immortalized on vinyl and emblazoned on my cerebral cortex.

They were cool for a while, but when many of the other kids outgrew them, I remained loyal. That's a tendency of mine. It can be either a virtue or a character flaw, depending on the object of that loyalty. In some cases, it's perseverance. In others, it amounts to banging my head against a brick wall.

As far as KISS is concerned, I'll let you be the judge about which activity I'm engaged in. They're no longer my favorite band, but I still buy all the music they put out. I saw them in concert for the third time this year, and I offer no apologies for standing on my feet and headbanging with the best of them, just as I did when I was 15 years young.

But I can't say they're my heroes anymore. I can't say anyone really is — not even the people you'll read about in the pages ahead, as much as I admire what many of them have accomplished. To me, heroes are two-dimensional demigods who make things seem effortless and accomplish feats to which ordinary mortals could never aspire.

I briefly considered *Heroes* as the title for this book, but then I realized it's not about those kind of people ... because those kind of people don't exist. It's about ordinary human beings who found themselves, through no fault of their own, in extraordinarily difficult situations. It's about people who might have been described as victims of persecution, bullying and repression — except for the fact that they refused to be victims.

Some of the people you'll meet in the pages ahead aren't necessarily folks you'd want to emulate. A Tibetan student set himself on fire. An adventurer and animal-lover subjected herself to blizzard conditions and bone-chilling temperatures over hundreds of miles of frozen wilderness.

Not once.

Not twice.

But 17 times.

Each of these people had their failings. I have no intention of putting them up on some high pedestal and turning them into monuments that are destined to crumble. Exactly the opposite: I want to preserve the vitality of what they accomplished as very fallible human beings who overcame adversity — sometimes despite the longest of odds.

Many readers will find something to criticize about the choices I made here. Believe it or not, I think that's a good thing, because the subjects I profile in this volume were selected for their diversity. The message is simply this: No matter your race, gender, sexual orientation, ethnic background, religion or nationality, you just might, at some point in time, find yourself on the receiving end of prejudice. You can't escape it by being a Christian, by practicing magic, by following the "proper" social norms or being the right skin color.

No matter who you are, there may come a time when you are in the minority and subject to ridicule.

When you are the underdog.

In fact, the original title for this book was *Underdogs*, but I realized that wasn't where I wanted to put all my focus. I didn't want this book to be about the long odds human beings sometimes face, but about how they manage to beat those odds. I remembered being bullied as a child, and I thought to myself, "What if I were to write a book about people who had been bullied, persecuted or worse — for whatever reason — and how they managed to come out on top despite it all?" Those are the kind of stories, I suspected, that people just might want to read.

So I went looking for them.

And I found them in both the past and the present, which are represented just about equally here. I found them in the stories of Native Americans, women, African-Americans, Roma and Armenians. In stories of slavery in the South Pacific and apartheid in South Africa. In tales of people wrongfully accused on the 1950s blacklists , in 17th century Massachusetts and 20th century Connecticut. In the lives of sports heroes, political activists and people who simply made a difference though their sacrifice and courage.

50 UNDEFEATED

The people profiled in this book aren't all historical giants. I tended to avoid the obvious choices — the Martin Luther Kings, the Dalai Lamas, the Susan B. Anthonys, Cesar Chavezes, Salman Rushdies and the Nelson Mandelas. Instead, I went looking off the beaten track for people who might be somewhat less than famous but whose stories resonate just as strongly with those who celebrate the human spirit in its fight to overcome bigotry and oppression.

Well-known names will pop up from time to time. I thought the story of Jackie Robinson breaking baseball's color barrier was too well known to repeat here, but I was fascinated to find his name surface in connection with others who overcame similar obstacles around the same time. The stories of Rosa Parks and Malala Yousafzai were just too good to pass up.

No, not everyone here is famous, and not everyone here is perfect, either. Let me rephrase that: All the people profiled in this book are *not* perfect. The purpose of the volume isn't to glorify or exalt *them*. It's to inspire *you*, the reader. No triumph comes without some measure of loss, whether it be in the form of noble sacrifice or unbidden sorrow. There are plenty of both in the pages ahead. But there is also plenty of hope, courage, strength and perseverance — the qualities that make these stories truly special.

And inspiring.

I hope you find as much fulfillment reading them as I did in writing them.

Ceija Stoika
Highway to Hell

When she was 8 years old, Ceija Stojka was taken to Auschwitz. She wasn't Jewish, but to the Nazis, she was something just as bad.

She was Roma.

In what became known to some as the *Porajmos* — devouring or destruction — the Nazis undertook a systematic program of ethnic cleansing in order to rid the earth of the Roma, whom they declared were "enemies of the race-based state." During World War II estimates suggest that between 220,000 and 1.5 million Roma were slaughtered.

The Germans didn't call them Roma. They referred to them derisively as gypsies, a term most among the Roma find offensive and one that certainly isn't accurate. It stems from a false belief that the Roma were originally from Egypt, and thence were referred to as "Egypcien" — a term that became shortened to read gypsy. In fact, they seem to have migrated to Europe from a different direction entirely, their original homeland being central India.

Some of the Roma did, indeed, embrace a semi-nomadic lifestyle, traveling in caravans that stopped periodically to set up tent camps. They often earned their living as tinkers, coppersmiths, horse traders, the last of these occupations being favored by Stojka's family. Her parents would often take her to New Vienna, a city south of the Austrian capital and site of a horse market where "Roma from near and far" would gather.

"Our parents worked the trailers behind (New Vienna)," she said. "We tied the horses to a nut tree or cherry tree and picked up hay from the farmers. We would spend five, six days there, until the horse market took place. We children enjoyed going there with our fathers — they would trade and sell horses with the farmers there."

Many Roma live in large extended families, and Stojka's Lovara clan was no exception. There were some 200 people in her clan, and she was the fifth of six children. Her family made do with what they had: on one occasion, her father made her a skirt using some material he had salvaged from a broken lampshade.

He would not live to see her grow up.

"One day, the Gestapo arrested our father, Karl Wacker Horvath, at our home," she said. "They came in a small car and pushed him inside. We children stood there, crying for our father. He winked once more and then they drove him away. That was 1941 and it's my last memory of him. We never saw him again."

She recalled that "a few months later, my mother received his ashes in a box."

They took her sister next and then forced the entire family to move to a camp for the Roma at Auschwitz/Birkenau, where they "lived in the shadows of a smoking crematorium" and called the path in front of their barracks "the highway to hell" because it led to the gas chambers.

Stojka and her mother and sisters later managed to convince the Nazis to take them to Bergen-Belsen concentration camp. There, she survived by following her mother's advice to eat anything she could find, whether it was grass, bark, leather or even dirt. The one thing she refused to eat were the corpses that she saw around her every day.

Others did. It was all they could do to stay alive one more day.

On arriving at the camp, Stojka recalled, she saw two piles of dead bodies. "They had not been dead long. I touched them and felt their warmth. I asked their forgiveness and buried myself in the bodies to try to stay warm."

It was that cold.

But she survived, and British forces finally liberated her from the camp on April 15, 1945 along with more than 50,000 other prisoners, many of them ill and emaciated. When the 11th Armored Division arrived, they also found some 13,000 corpses strewn across the grounds of the camp, unburied.

Stojka's mother found a wheelbarrow and wheeled her an astonishing 700 miles from Bergen to Linz, where extended family would gather once a year. But from among the 200 members of her clan who had lived together before the war, just a handful were found to have survived: Stojka, her siblings, an aunt and her mother. Of the 11,000 Roma living in prewar Austria, only 2,000 lived through the carnage.

The Nazi persecution was nothing new for the Roma, who had long been branded as con artists, distrusted as drifters and used as scapegoats. Austrian Emperor Leopold I declared the Roma outlaws twice, in 1697 and again four years later. A few years after that, it was decreed that all Roma men were to be hanged; the women and boys were to be flogged and sent into exile.

So it is no surprise that the fall of Nazi Germany failed to end the persecution of the Roma, who were ordered expelled from Austria just three years later. Behind the Iron Curtain, governments sought to break up what was left of their extended families and force them into low-paying factory and menial jobs. Czechoslovakia outlawed their nomadic lifestyle in 1958, and Poland did the same six years later.

In an effort to complete the ethnic cleansing the Nazis had started, Czechoslovakia offered often-destitute Roma women money to undergo sterilization procedures. In 1987, just 2 percent of the nation's population were Roma, but more than a third of Roma women were sterilized.

Western Europe also took a dim view of the Roma. France deported 10,000 Roma to Romania and Bulgaria in 2009 and more than 8,000 more the following year, citing "illicit trafficking, deeply unworthy living conditions and exploitation of children for begging, prostitution and crime." Smaller numbers were deported from Sweden and Denmark.

Through much of this continued discrimination, Stojka and her family persevered. Stojka started making trinkets to sell and saved enough money that she was able, nine years later, to buy a small place to live.

It was not until some four decades later that she would publish her autobiography. Her father had been a writer, and now she would follow in his footsteps. Shortly afterward, she started drawing and painting, using just the materials at hand — her fingers, toothpicks, pieces of cardboard, glass jars: "I work with everything that comes between my fingers."

Some of her works recall the cruelty and oppression of life in Nazi Germany: her mother staring out from behind barbed wire; a dancing caricature of Adolf Hitler. Others offer glimpses into the Roma life: a wagon parked in the snow; two Roma dancing by moonlight; a Roma woman in a flowing pink dress carrying a basket and flowers across a field into a colorfully drawn Roma encampment.

In 2009, she brought her works to the United States for the first time, exhibiting them in Vermont, Oregon and Sonoma State University in California.

Her writing and art remind the world of what she and her people have endured, and challenge them to keep remembering. "I am afraid that Europe is forgetting its past," she said, "and that Auschwitz is only sleeping."

"I, Ceija, say Auschwitz lives and breathes still in me today."

— Ceija Stojka

Larry Doby
Second to None

He broke baseball's color barrier. The reason you may not remember him is that he was the second person to do so. Doby became the first African-American to play in the American League, less than three months *after* Jackie Robinson started playing for the Dodgers in the National League.

The date was July 5, 1947, not all that long ago.

Still, "No one remembers Larry Doby," Brooklyn Assemblyman Hakeem Jeffries said.

But they should. Doby didn't play in the Big Apple, as Robinson did, under the glare of the lights and publicity that routinely shone on Ebbetts Field. He was off in Cleveland, where Bill Veeck (as in "wreck"), a man known for his publicity stunts, owned the Indians. Veeck once hired a professional clown as a coach and signed 3-foot, 7-inch circus performer Eddie Gaedel for his biggest asset: a diminutive strike zone. Gaedel drew a walk on four straight pitches in his only plate appearance.

But Doby was no clown. He was the real thing. Few people remember him, even though he faced the same challenges Robinson did. He didn't stay in the same hotel with the rest of the team during spring training, and he was a target of racial slurs from fans and other players alike during his first season with the team.

"It was not always easy for Larry," said Frank Lautenberg, who attended Eastside High School with Doby in Paterson, N.J., and went on to a life of accomplishment himself as a U.S. senator. "He was forced to eat in separate restaurants, to sleep in separate hotels. Some teammates wouldn't even shake his hand. But he pressed on."

Even some of the game's biggest names ridiculed him.

"Bill Veeck did the Negro race no favor when he signed Larry Doby to a Cleveland contract," Hall of Famer Rogers Hornsby quipped after seeing Doby play. "If Veeck wanted to demonstrate that the Negro has no place in major league baseball, he could have used no subtler means to establish the point. If he were white he wouldn't be considered good enough to play with a semi-pro club."

To Hornsby, Doby was just another one of Veeck's stunts. It's no wonder that Hornsby never matched his success on the field as either a scout or a manager. He obviously didn't know talent, which Doby had in abundance.

Doby himself admitted that it was "very tough" when he joined the Indians and that others on the team refused to even acknowledge him because of his race. "I'd never faced any circumstances like that. Teammates were lined up, and some would greet you and some wouldn't. You could deal with it, but it was hard."

It was worse, of course, in the South. In those days, there weren't any big league teams in Dixie, but teams would play occasional exhibition games there. For one such game, against the New York Giants in Texarkana, Doby was refused taxi service because of his race and had to walk to the ballpark. Once he got there, the gatekeepers initially refused to let him in, despite his uniform.

Indians manager Lou Boudreau finally arrived and escorted him past a hostile all-white crowd and into the stadium ... where he was subject to still more abuse. Boudreau had to take him out of the game after the fifth inning because racist fans were throwing bottles and other debris at him from the stands.

As Franklin Lewis of the Cleveland Press put it, he was a "six hour ball player per day" and "an 18-hour Jim Crow personality the rest of the time."

But when he was on the field, Doby made quite an impression.

He was the first black player to hit one out of the park in both the World Series and the All-Star Game. He was so good that, in 1954 he led the American League in home runs (32) and runs batted in (126). He finished second in voting for the league's Most Valuable Player and helped Cleveland win more games that year than any other team before or since. He made six consecutive All-Star teams and was eventually voted into baseball's Hall of Fame.

Notably, Doby wasn't just the second African-American player in the majors, he became the second African-American manager as well when he was hired by the Chicago White Sox in 1978. He was also the first African-American to play in a major professional basketball league.

The same year he joined the Indians, Doby suited up for the Paterson Crescents in the American Basketball League. Few people know about that one. Few people have probably even heard of the ABL, but it was the first major pro basketball league in America. Doby — who had once accepted a *basketball* scholarship to Long Island University — played in eight games for his hometown Paterson Crescents, scoring 15 points.

In some ways, Doby didn't just help pave the way for players like Willie Mays and Barry Bonds, he also helped open doors for NBA superstars like Michael Jordan and Kobe Bryant. He retained his interest in the sport throughout his life, and from 1983 until 1990 served as director of community affairs for the New Jersey (now Brooklyn) Nets.

"He was a great American," Hall of Fame pitcher Bob Feller said. "He served the country in World War II and was a great ballplayer. He was kind of like Buzz Aldrin, the second man on the moon, because he was the second African-American player in the majors."

50 UNDEFEATED

*"I knew being accepted was going to be hard,
but I knew I was involved in a situation
that was going to bring opportunities to blacks."*
— Larry Doby

George Takei
Taking the Helm

One of the main characters in the play *Allegiance* is elected president at his high school — just before being sent away to a relocation center as part of the Japanese American internment during World War II.

He had big dreams.

It wasn't quite the same for the man behind this moving musical that opened in San Diego's Old Globe Theatre in the fall of 2012, but there are a few similarities. He was, like the character, elected student body president, but it came after the time he spent at the Rohwer and Tule Lake relocation centers during the war. And unlike the character — an older version of whom he played in the production — he doesn't seem bitter. Rather, he seems passionate that this story be told and not forgotten.

It's a moving story that examines the question of allegiance. Should it be tested — or trusted? Does a nation owe its citizens the same allegiance it expects to receive from them? To whom (or what) do we owe our primary allegiance: our dreams, our family or our country? And how should we express it?

All these questions are raised during the course of the play. They're the sort of ethical debates one often saw in episodes of the *Star Trek* television series, which dealt with such issues as racism, military intervention and cultural bias. Yet in *Allegiance*, they're not part of some abstract future, they're part of our shared history — and part of the history of the man behind this particular enterprise, George Takei.

Takei might be best remembered for his role as helmsman Hikaru Sulu on *Star Trek*, but if there's any justice, his role in bringing *Allegiance* to the stage will have the greatest lasting impact. Many people are familiar with Takei's popular page on the social networking site Facebook. What they may not be familiar with is the fact that he set up that page specifically to promote *Allegiance* — more than a year before the show debuted.

In the musical's souvenir program, he described his family's experience of being taken forcibly removed from their home. "I was five years old when armed soldiers came and banged on the front door of our Los Angeles home and ordered us out," he recalled. "I remember my mother had tears rolling down her cheeks. The terror of that morning is indelibly seared into my memory."

Takei remembered other things too. He recalled seeing his neighbors gather around anxiously as he and his family were being taken away, waiting until they were gone for the chance to loot their belongings. He also remembered being taken to a temporary relocation site and living in a horse stable for several weeks while waiting for transfer to a more permanent internment camp in Rohwer, Ark.

There was a barbed-wire fence.

A searchlight.

The humidity and the mosquitoes that bred in a nearby swamp.

Sentry towers staffed by guards armed with machine guns.

It's not as though the internees were well cared-for. The government spent just 48 cents a day to feed them, and they weren't allowed to have the utensils necessary to cook for themselves. There was no plumbing, and "home" was a barracks whose insulation consisted of tarpaper.

As a child, however, Takei adapted quickly and came to view life in the camp as just his everyday routine. He hadn't been alive long enough to know much else.

"Because I was a child, I didn't understand the depth of the degradation and deprivation my parents suffered," he said in an interview years later, "or how courageous my mother had been to smuggle a sewing machine into camp, which permitted her to make modest curtains for our bare quarters."

Takei's family was just one of thousands affected when President Franklin Roosevelt signed Executive order 9066, forcing Japanese Americans on the West Coast from their homes and ordering them locked up in 10 "relocation centers" spread across seven states from California to Wyoming to Arkansas.

It's less widely known, but a similar order was given in Canada, which established a 100-mile-wide coastal zone in British Columbia where people of Japanese descent were forbidden. Japanese language schools and newspapers were forced to close, and Japanese-Canadian fishing boats were impounded. Then, 23,000 Canadians of Japanese descent were carted off and imprisoned at camps in British Columbia. The homes and businesses they left behind were auctioned off by the government.

In at least one respect, the situation was even worse in Canada than in America: Japanese men were separated from their families and sent off to perform manual labor.

Among them was David Suzuki, who like Takei was interned as a child and later became student body president at his school. "My drive to do well has been motivated by the desire to demonstrate to my fellow Canadians that my family and I had not deserved to be treated as we were," Suzuki said.

To say Suzuki has done well in life would be an understatement. He earned a doctorate in zoology from the University of Chicago in 1961 and became not only a scientist but also a fixture on radio and television. There, he drew upon his background in science to give audiences a greater understanding of the natural world. He became advocate for wildlife preservation, sustainability and climate change awareness.

"The human brain now holds the key to our future," he would say. "We have to recall the image of the planet from outer space: a single entity in which air, water and continents are interconnected. That is our home."

Takei, like Suzuki, went on to become a fixture on television and could say a thing or two about viewing Earth from the perspective of outer space.

When the war ended, his family returned to Los Angeles, where he had been born. It was there that he served as student body president at Mount Vernon Junior High and became involved in Boy Scouts. He initially went to college at UC Berkeley, where he studied architecture, but returned to Los Angeles and majored in theater at UCLA.

He once asked him why his father hadn't protected him from the internment, accusing him of leading their family like sheep to the slaughter. Takei remembered the sorrow in his father's eyes when he answered, "Maybe you're right," then turned and disappeared into his bedroom.

"I will always regret those words," Takei said. "The tragedy of the internment of 120,000 Japanese Americans was not only that it was the greatest violation of our constitutional guarantees, but that it broke apart families and whole communities, and left scars that today remain unhealed, even after the government later apologized and issued reparations."

It's no accident that those family fractures and scars are a central theme of *Allegiance*.

Takei received his master's degree in 1964, and two years later found himself about as far away from an internment camp as you could get. By this time, he was off exploring the galaxy on a huge starship that could travel nine times the speed of light.

Well, at least on TV.

Indeed, most people probably know Takei for his role as Sulu, which he played for three seasons in the 1960s and reprised in several motion pictures. It was a groundbreaking role in many ways, with

Sulu serving as part of an ethnically diverse crew that included officers of African, Russian, Asian and — yes — Vulcan descent. It seems to have been a perfect fit for Takei, whose diverse career extended far beyond the Star Trek universe and into the realms of activism, politics and humor.

After the series was canceled following a three-year run, Takei tried his hand at politics, running for Los Angeles City Council and losing by fewer than two thousand votes. He testified before a congressional commission on the Japanese American internment and donated the money he received for reparations to the Japanese American National Museum.

He donated $10,000 more after he and husband Brad Altman won an episode of television's *Newlywed Game*.

Not only was Takei the first Japanese American helmsman to serve on a starship (now that's a distinction!), he and Altman became the first same-sex couple to apply for a marriage license in West Hollywood, California. They were married in September 2008, three years after Takei confirmed his sexual orientation.

"As a gay actor, it would have been suicidal" to come out during his early career, he said. "I was in the closet throughout."

His decision to come out as gay came after California Gov. Arnold Schwarzenegger vetoed a bill that would have legalized same-sex marriage. "That night I was watching the news, and I saw all these young people on Santa Monica Boulevard out protesting," he recalled. "I was with them in terms of the blood that was boiling in me, but I was home comfortable. I knew I had to come out publicly. To the press."

Takei hasn't made things all that comfortable for opponents of same-sex marriage since then. If his blood is boiling, however, it's seldom evident. Takei advocates for same-sex marriage with the same good humor that has made him an effective spokesperson for other causes throughout his career.

His wit can be disarming.

50 UNDEFEATED

When pro basketball player Tim Hardaway said, "I hate gay people" in 2007, Takei recorded a tongue-in-cheek public service announcement "on behalf of gay people everywhere" stating, "we like you very much."

Where's Tim Hardaway now? He retired two years later and has apologized for his statement. As of this writing, his unofficial Facebook fan page had nearly 7,500 "likes."

Takei's had nearly 2.8 million.

It's easy to tell where the fans' allegiance lies.

"It's really hard to hate someone for being different when you're too busy laughing together."

— George Takei

Mary Parsons
Toil and Trouble

Those who live in poverty often find themselves repressed by the upper classes, but even the wealthy can find themselves targets for discrimination.

There are times when the hoi polloi practice their own brand of prejudice against the well-to-do aristocrats on their expansive estates. And sometimes, when this occurs, the most sophisticated home security system may not be able to protect them.

Burglar alarms.

Iron gates.

Trip wires.

Satellite systems.

No such security measures were in place in the 17th century, when 8-year-old Mary Bliss crossed the Atlantic Ocean with her parents and settled in Hartford, Conn. Born into a prominent and distinguished English family, she married well, settling down with a successful merchant named Joseph Parsons. Together, they moved to Springfield and started a family.

Mary Bliss Parsons had three children before a new opportunity arose about 20 miles to the north along the Connecticut River. Settlers from Springfield bought up the bulk of land that would become Northampton, Mass., in the wake of a smallpox epidemic that had decimated the Algonquin population of the area. Among those settlers was the Parsons family.

According to local tradition, Mary was somewhat standoffish, as members of the upper crust often appeared to those beneath them on the economic ladder. "Possessed of great beauty and talents," she was nonetheless described as a person of "haughty manners" who was "not very amiable" and "exclusive in her choice of associates."

It wasn't long before she became the target of certain disturbing accusations. Two years after the couple's arrival in Northampton, she and a fellow resident named Sarah Bridgman both became pregnant. Sarah and her husband James, like the Parsonses, had been married in Hartford and moved to Springfield before ultimately settling in Northampton around 1654.

Like Mary, Sarah had been born in England.

The similarities, however, ended there.

John and Mary Parsons' new life in Northampton seemed to be off to an auspicious start when she gave birth to a healthy baby boy. Not long afterward, Sarah Bridgman gave birth to a son of her own — only to watch him die just two weeks later. And she soon became convinced, at least publicly, that Mary Parsons was to blame for her misfortune.

What it all boiled down to, it seemed, was a case of jealousy. Sarah was soon heard complaining about the good fortune that seemed to follow the Parsons family around. Not only were Joseph and Mary well off, they had already been blessed with three healthy children. Now Mary Parsons had given birth to a fourth child — a healthy baby boy — while Sarah Bridgman's son had been born sickly and perished as an infant.

There was something unnatural about it.

Well, actually, there wasn't. The infant mortality rate for the time in colonial New England was somewhere between 10 and 30 percent, and it was hardly unusual for a child to die shortly after birth. Still, Sarah Bridgman seemed to have seized on what she perceived to be the unfairness of it all and began spreading the notion that Mary Parsons owed her good fortune to a deal with the devil.

Joseph Parsons, outraged that his wife was being falsely — and publicly — vilified, took matters into his own hands and decided to sue Sarah Bridgman for slander. It was a potentially hazardous move, as he risked the possibility that Sarah Bridgman would turn the tables on Mary by airing her accusations in open court. And, indeed, she tried to do just that.

Bridgman related a suitably spooky occurrence shortly after giving birth during which she heard a "great blow at the door" and noticed that her child had changed. Then, looking through a hole in the door, she saw "two women pass by the door with white clothes on their heads; then I concluded my child would die indeed." The mysterious women then disappeared, convincing Bridgman that "there (was) wickedness in the place."

Such accusations were par for the course at witchcraft trials. Accusers would routinely report seeing disembodied spirits — supposedly either belonging to or controlled by the accused — appear as a harbinger of some evil deed. In this case, such an apparition served as a portent of the newborn's death.

Further witnesses were also called, and another woman reported that she had spun a ball of yarn for Mary Parsons that wound up all in knots. Since she had no similar problems spinning yarn for anyone else, she concluded that this particular stretch of yarn had been the unfortunate victim of Mary's supposed witchcraft.

Other coincidences were introduced into evidence as well. One woman's daughter supposedly became ill after Mary passed by. A man had words with her one day, and the next found his cow so sick it was "ready to die."

Similar evidence was enough to convict and execute some 20 people four decades later in Salem, 120 miles to the east. In this case, however, Mary Parsons had enough witnesses of her own to cast significant doubt on Sarah Bridgman's allegations. Besides, as the plaintiff in the case, she was accorded greater credibility (plaintiffs in court cases at the time generally fared better than defendants).

Several people put the lie to Bridgman's story by testifying that her child had been sick from birth, and a neighbor told the court that Parsons had nothing to do with the death of the earlier witness' cow. In fact, the animal had died of "water in the belly."

The court found in favor of Parsons and ordered the Bridgmans to either issue a public apology or pay a fine. Indignantly, they refused to acknowledge any fault and instead paid the money — which should have been the end of it.

But it wasn't.

Nearly two decades later, the Bridgman family renewed its witchcraft accusations against Mary Parsons, who was by this time about 46 years old. Again, the occasion was a sudden death in the Bridgman family — this time, Sarah's daughter, also named Mary — and this time the case was brought against her by the deceased's widower.

Mary Parsons was once again called into court, this time as the defendant against an indictment that alleged she had "entered into familiarity with the Devil and committed several acts of witchcraft." She was physically examined for evidence of so-called witch's teats (protrusions on the body such as moles, from which demonic imps were thought to nurse), and was ultimately acquitted of the charges.

Mary Parsons and her husband ultimately left Northampton and returned to Springfield, with their son Samuel staying behind on the property. Joseph died four years later, and Mary passed away in 1712 at the age of 85, nearly two decades after the more famous Salem witch craze, during which accusations were brought against about 150 people. There, too, the underlying cause was not witchcraft, but rather family feuds, economic rivalries and petty jealousies.

That was three centuries ago.

One might have thought the lesson had been learned. Yet even today, witch hunts continue to provide an excuse for bringing legal action against innocent people and, in some cultures, forcing them into exile and branding them with what amounts to a scarlet letter for life.

Consider the following:

In California in the late 20th century, several day-care center workers were hauled into court on various charges of satanic ritual abuse of children. Only a handful of the charges ever produced convictions, but one of the cases, the McMartin preschool trial, lasted seven years. It went down in history as the most expensive criminal trial in U.S. history with a price tag of $15 million. Another case in Kern County produced convictions that were later overturned after several of the witnesses recanted.

Today, in the West African country of Ghana, women are routinely accused of witchcraft. There are no trials. The accusations themselves are generally sufficient to force the women into remote and squalid "witch villages" — exile camps where they are frequently abused and given no hope of ever seeing their families again.

Children themselves are increasingly being branded as witches, especially in African communities (both on the continent itself and abroad). These children are subjected to exorcisms, torture and even death for their alleged sorcery.

On Christmas Day 2010, the body of 15-year-old Kristy Bamu was found mutilated on the bathroom floor of a London high-rise apartment. Football coach Eric Bikubi and his girlfriend Magalie Bamu — Kristy's brother — were found guilty of murdering him because they suspected him of witchcraft.

And in some ways, the effects of the 17th century witchcraft trials linger even today. In 2012, a group of activists, including some descended from 11 people convicted of witchcraft in 17th century Connecticut, is calling on the state to pardon them. These activists have taken their case to the legislature, the governor and even the queen of England (under whose jurisdiction the trials were conducted). Though the trials took place about the same time as the Parsons case and little more than a stone's throw away across the state line, none of the authorities petitioned has granted the request. The governor said it wasn't in his power under the state constitution, and the queen said the cases would have to be re-examined all over again ... even though the evidence was nearly 400 years old.

Clearly, the hysteria that surrounded the witchcraft accusations against Mary Parsons is anything but a thing of the past. But despite the animosity that existed between the Parsons and Bridgman families in the 17th century, all that seems to be water under the bridge now. Members of both families still live within a few miles of each other in Northampton, site of a family feud that has apparently, and blissfully run its course.

"The jury brought in their verdict. They found her not guilty. And so she was discharged."

— Court reader in Mary Parsons' 1674 trial

Aesha Mohammadzai
Time to Heal

Aesha Mohammadzai was just 18 years old. Had she lived in the United States, she would have just become eligible to vote. But she didn't live in America. She lived halfway across the world in Afghanistan. And it was at the age of 18 that she was subjected to one of the most horrific and brutal acts of torture imaginable. Her nose and ears were cut off ... by her husband's family.

She hadn't necessarily wanted to marry the man in the first place, but she hadn't been given a choice.

Aesha, often referred to as Bibi ("Lady") Aesha, was just a girl when her father promised her hand in marriage to a member of the Taliban movement in Afghanistan. He delivered her as compensation because one of her family members had killed someone in a Taliban family.

For the next few years she endured continual abuse, forced to sleep with animals and beaten repeatedly, until she finally escaped with the aid of two neighbors she thought would help her. Instead, they took her to Kandahar Province — a Taliban stronghold — and tried to sell her to a different man. Police eventually caught up with her and took her into custody. Then they returned her to her abusers.

As punishment for bringing shame to her husband's family, they mutilated her face. That way, no one else would want her.

They took her into the mountains, and the local Taliban commander watched as this young woman, shivering with cold and fright, pleaded for mercy. Instead, they shone flashlights in her face, blinding her to the grisly form of "justice" they soon inflicted on her.

Her father-in-law held a gun to her head, and her brother-in-law held her down while her husband sliced off her nose. Then he showed it off like a trophy around town. After that, they dumped her in the mountains and left her there to die. She managed, however, to crawl to her grandfather's house, and she was taken a U.S. medical facility. She stayed there for ten weeks, and her story eventually came to the attention of *The Daily Beast* online newspaper.

From there, she was photographed for the cover of *Time* magazine, her disfigured face used to graphically illustrate the headline "What Happens if We Leave Afghanistan."

Then she came to the United States.

Aesha, who was illiterate before leaving Afghanistan, started to learn English and began making beaded jewelry. She was fitted with a prosthetic nose at West Hills Hospital in California but grew tired of it and stopped wearing it. She wound up living in New York and, later, moved to Maryland, where she began living with a family in a town home about an hour outside Washington, D.C.

There is no happy ending here — how can there be with the abuse Aesha has endured? She has struggled to find peace, connections and a place in American society. The husband who disfigured her has never been found, and only one person has ever been arrested in connection with the brutal crimes against her: her father-in-law.

He was set free after six months.

But Aesha is alive and she has a chance. Considering what she has been through, that in itself is beyond remarkable.

"When they cut off my nose and ears, I passed out. … I opened my eyes, and I couldn't even see because of all the blood."

— Aesha Mohammadzai

50 UNDEFEATED

Susan Boyle

Dream Come True

Which musical artist created Britain's fastest-selling debut CD of all time?

The Beatles, surely.

Nope.

Oasis?

Guess again.

Queen. It's got to be Queen.

Nice try.

Freddie Mercury had some great pipes, to be sure, but many would argue that Susan Boyle's are even better. As for Lennon and McCartney, well, they were a great team when it came to composing music, but they can only imagine singing this well.

Boyle became an overnight sensation after she appeared on a TV show called *Britain's Got Talent* in a dark cream lace dress at the age of 47 and was met with notoriously finicky judge Simon Cowell and a visual chorus of eye rolls from judges and audience alike. Her hair was, as she calls it, fuzzy. And she didn't look the part of your typical aspiring pop-star chanteuse, to be sure.

Then she started to sing.

Within the first few notes, the rolled eyes had given way first to raised eyebrows, then just as quickly to smiles and applause. By the end of her rendition of *I Dreamed a Dream*, the audience was standing on its feet. Judge Piers Morgan labeled it "stunning, an incredible performance."

Boyle didn't win the competition (she finished second), but just one clip of her initial performance went on to be viewed more than 16 million times on YouTube — and counting. And her debut album, bearing the title of the song she sang that first night, debuted atop both the United Kingdom and U.S. album charts.

Before that day, she had never been out on a date.

Boyle had grown up in Scotland, the youngest of nine children born to a factory worker and a shorthand typist. Deprived of oxygen at birth, she had to cope with a learning disability and endured teasing at school, where she was tagged with the derisive nickname "Susie Simple."

"I was called names because of my fuzzy hair and because I struggled in class," she told *The Daily Mail*. " I told the teachers but, because it was more verbal than physical, I could never prove anything. But words often hurt more than cuts and bruises, and the scars are still there."

It happened when she was 17, and a gang of girls teased her relentlessly to the point that she considered suicide. She sought professional help and underwent treatment.

"In my case, it was a small group of teenage girls that put me to that place," she remembered. "They're the worst kind. It can really hold you back and damage you. Mental bullying is the worst kind of bullying."

And it wasn't just other children. Boyle said she received corporal punishment on a daily basis at her school. "There was discipline for the sake of discipline back then, and you are looking at someone who would get the belt every day. 'Will you shut up, Susan! Whack!" she said. "There's nothing worse than another person having power over you by bullying you and you not knowing how to get rid of that thing."

After leaving school, she held only one job — as a trainee cook — that lasted just six months. From then on, she stayed home, supported by her parents and a stranger to romantic relationships. "I've never been kissed," she said in the *Daily Mail* interview. "If someone even pecked me on the cheek it would be nice, but I've never even got that close."

Her father died. Her siblings moved away. And she was left in the house with her mother, occasionally singing karaoke at local pubs. Boyle's only brush with the recording industry involved three tracks she recorded on a demo that she ended up sending to record companies and talent competitions in 1998. She used her entire savings to produce it.

No recording contract came of it, but her mother encouraged her to audition for *Britain's Got Talent* after she won a number of local singing competitions. Worried she was too old, she almost pulled out of the auditions, but her vocal coach persuaded her to go through with it as a tribute to her mother, who had since passed away. When she took the stage that first night, it marked her first public singing appearance since her mother's death.

Since her triumphant turn on Britain's Got Talent, Boyle has recorded four CDs. In April 2012, she performed at Windsor Castle for Queen Elizabeth II's diamond jubilee pageant.

"Another dream ticked off my wish list!" she wrote on her website. "To say it was an honour is an understatement."

Most anyone who's heard her sing would probably agree that the honour is all ours.

"Modern society is too quick to judge people on their appearances. There is not much you can do about it; it is the way they think; it is the way they are. But maybe this could teach them a lesson, or set an example."

— Susan Boyle

Glenn Burke

The High-Five Guy

I didn't realize it at the time, but I saw the first high-five in sports history.

It was the last game of the 1977 baseball season, and three members of the Los Angeles Dodgers had hit 30 home runs: Reggie Smith, Ron Cey and Steve Garvey. A fourth guy on the squad, outfielder Dusty Baker, had 29. When he stepped to the plate that afternoon, no four players on one team had ever hit 30 home runs in the same season. I was there at Dodger Stadium, standing in front of my seat along the right-field foul line, waiting to see whether Baker would come through.

Sure enough, he went deep. And I, a 14-year-old Dodgers fan, went nuts. Everyone was cheering, jumping up and down as we watched the ball clear the fence and Baker started circling the bases. Lost to me in that triumphant moment was the fact that another historic moment was about to occur as Baker approached home plate. Glenn Burke, the man in the on-deck circle, raised his hand to greet Baker as he completed his trip around the bases.

"His hand was up in the air, and he was arching way back," Baker said later. "So I reached up and hit his hand. It seemed like the thing to do."

In that moment, history was made. As far as anyone knows, it was the first high-five ever at a sporting event. Me? I didn't notice it. The funny thing is, I wasn't even aware that I'd been present for the occasion until I began doing research for this book. The research had nothing to do with Baker's history-making home run or even the high-five. It had to do with Burke, who made a very different kind of history — he was the first openly gay player in Major League Baseball.

When Burke came up to the majors, the buzz wasn't about his sexual orientation but his ability. He could have been a pro basketball player. At an even 6 feet tall, he reportedly could dunk two-handed. But that was just for show. More impressively, he led Berkeley High School to an undefeated season and was named the Northern California High School Player of the Year for basketball in 1970.

Burke, however, chose to pursue a career in baseball, and his athletic ability had some observers touting him as the next Willie Mays. That in itself would have been enough to live up to. But Burke soon found he was supposed to live up to another expectation, as well — he was supposed to be (or at least appear to be) straight. This was before the AIDS crisis, which revealed to the public that the dashing movie star Rock Hudson had been gay. It was just before openly gay candidate Harvey Milk got elected supervisor in San Francisco. And L.A., was certainly *not* San Francisco.

"Being gay at the that time was a kiss of death for a ballplayer," teammate Reggie Smith said.

When Al Campanis, the Dodgers' general manager, found out about Burke's sexual orientation, Burke wrote in his autobiography, he offered $75,000 to pay for a honeymoon if Burke got married. "I guess you mean to a woman," Burke quipped in declining the offer. The response did not go over well, especially considering that Burke had struck up a friendship with the gay son of manager Tommy Lasorda.

It wasn't long before Burke found himself traded to the Oakland Athletics after just two seasons with the Dodgers. Oakland was closer to home, but his treatment there was, if anything, even worse. According to new teammate Claudell Washington, A's manager Billy

Martin introduced Burke in the clubhouse by saying, "Oh, by the way, this is Glenn Burke. He's a faggot."

According to Mike Norris, a pitcher with the A's at the time, "The tension in the clubhouse was so thick you could cut it with a knife. Glenn was in a no-win situation. The best thing for him to do was retire."

And so, after less than two seasons with the A's, he did just that at the age of 27. Burke's childhood friend and sports agent Abdul-Jalil al-Hakim put it this way: "It was uncompromising on both ends. Glenn was comfortable with who he was; baseball was not comfortable with who he was."

A couple of years after leaving the majors, he let the fans know what most players already knew about his sexual orientation in an interview with *Inside Sports* magazine. "Prejudice drove me out of baseball sooner than I should have," he later told *The New York Times*, "but I wasn't changing."

He finished his major league career with a .237 batting average with 35 stolen bases and 38 runs batted in. Fifteen years after he left baseball, he was dead, struck down by the same HIV virus that had killed Hudson. But three decades after his last major league appearance, he was one of only two baseball players at that level to come out of the closet.

That would take a lot of guts today.

It took a hell of a lot more back then. Glenn Burke deserved that high-five, and a great deal more.

"They can't ever say now that a gay man can't play in the majors, because I'm a gay man and I made it."

— Glenn Burke

Walter Benjamin

Left, Write, Left

A correction that ran in *The Washington Post* on March 26, 2009, probably received little notice. Most of the people who read newspaper corrections are the ones who've been affected when the paper has gotten it wrong: Little League parents whose children's names have been misspelled or service clubs who want to correct an erroneous meeting time or date.

This particular correction concerned an article about President Ronald Reagan, who by the time it was printed had been out of office for more than two decades and who had passed away five years earlier.

One doesn't normally think of Reagan as someone who had to overcome prejudice. His life was one success story after another: Hollywood leading man, president of the Screen Actors Guild, two-term California governor and two-term president of the United States.

Reagan had a lot of charisma. My father, a professor who served for a time as the chairman of the California State University Academic Senate, invited Reagan — then governor of California — to speak to that body back in the early 1970s. Reagan, a Republican, wasn't too popular among generally liberal faculty representatives, but he won them over: "He came in to tepid applause and left to a standing ovation," my father told me. That was Ronald Reagan. The Great Communicator.

Though not in Reagan's class, my father was a pretty decent communicator, too. He was on a champion debate team in college, and he even ran for office. But it turns out he and Reagan had something else in common, too. This is where *The Washington Post* correction comes in. It addressed some confusion over Reagan had been right- or left-handed. Although he performed some functions with his left hand, he used his right hand when writing.

Joanne Drake, who served as Reagan's chief of staff after he left the White House, told *The Post* that she and others had "heard the president say he was born left-handed and was forced to learn to write with his right hand as a young child."

A schoolteacher once tried to do the same thing with my father, but he continued to use his left hand. Reagan, however, actually made the switch — though it appears he never fully adjusted. The man who would become the nation's 40th president never counted penmanship among his strengths. And he attributed this shortcoming to the fact that he was forced to switch from southpaw to righty when he wrote as a child. In a letter he wrote on his personalized Warner Bros. notepaper in 1942, he confessed, "Guess I don't write many letters 'cause I write a pretty bad hand. I sort of lay the blame on my parents, because they made me use my right hand and I was born left-handed."

Imagine someone forcing a pitcher like Sandy Koufax or Randy Johnson to throw right-handed. In baseball, you need a decent southpaw keep opponents on their toes. But somehow, it was fine for Lefty Grove to win 300 games and strike out hundreds of batters, but it wasn't OK for a kid like young Ronald Reagan to write with his left hand.

He wasn't alone.

About nine in every ten children born worldwide are right-handed, so lefties are definitely at a disadvantage. Common tools such as scissors, cameras, computer mice, guitars and golf clubs generally are made for right-handers. But because lefties aren't the "norm," they're often picked on — like just about any other minority. The word "left" even comes from an Anglo-Saxon word (*lyft*), which refers to something weak or broken. Worse still, the left hand historically has been linked to Satan, and the word "sinister" in Latin literally means something on the left side.

In the first part of the 20th century, some students were beaten for using their left hands. Others had their left arms tied to chairs to discourage their use. My father was lucky. When his first-grade teacher tried to convert him to right-handedness, his mother marched off to school the very next day and put a stop to it by confronting his teacher.

As it turns out, some research has shown that lefties aren't handicapped at all. Actually, they're more likely to be highly intelligent. Alan Searleman of St. Lawrence University in New York conducted a study that showed left-handers to have "higher 'fluid' intelligence and better vocabulary than the majority of the population."

He continued: "Although left-handed people had poorer memories, they were twice as good at all problem-solving tasks."

My father, a university professor emeritus, has an IQ of 140. He's in good company with even more accomplished left-handers: Wolfgang Amadeus Mozart, Bill Gates, Marie Curie, Isaac Newton, Leonardo da Vinci and Albert Schweitzer, to name a few. Reagan's in good company, as well, when it comes to the presidency — five of the past seven men who held the office were lefties.

So all that stuff about lefties being sinister and satanic? Forget about it.

But Sandy Koufax did have one wicked fastball.

50 UNDEFEATED

*"Strength lies in improvisation.
All the decisive blows are struck left-handed."*

— Walter Benjamin

Yarri
The Hero of Gundagai

In 1879, the local newspaper related an account from a certain visitor to Gundagai, a frontier town about 240 miles southwest of Sydney, Australia.

"A gentleman, who passed through South Gundagai on Monday, complains that he saw some individuals … maltreating and teasing an unfortunate blackfellow, whom he subsequently ascertained was Old Yarri."

The so-called blackfellow of whom they spoke was an Aboriginal Australian, a name applied to various peoples who lived on the continent before the first European settlers arrived in the late 18th century. Specifically, he was a member of the Wiradjuri, who lived on the Murrumbidgee floodplain where the European settlement of Gundagai was established in 1838.

No one deserved the kind of treatment meted out by these cruel individuals on that day in 1879, least of all Yarri.

He was, after all, a hero.

When European settlers came to the Gundagai region, they took from the Wiradjuri the land they had called home for centuries. At first, they put up temporary encampments on the flats between the Murrumbidgee River and its branch, Morley's Creek, but it wasn't long before they began to build permanent dwellings. The called their new home simply "The Crossing." They hadn't counted on the dangerous floods came when the river overflowed its banks.

The Wiradjuri tried to warn them.

The settlers wouldn't listen. Folk historian John Warner captured their attitude in his lyrics to *White Man Fool (Big Water Come Down)*, "Build an attic up in the rafters. Done in a day or so. We'll be safe upstairs when the river rises. What do the primitive natives know?"

Quite a bit, as it turns out. The settlers faced the true consequences of ignoring the Wiradjuris' warning on a June night in 1952, when a tremendous wall of water came barreling across the plain, forcing the town into a panic. The local pharmacist owned a small, flat-bottomed boat and saw a chance to profit from the calamity by hiring out his boat to rescue townsfolk caught in the floodwaters. The boat, however, proved no match for the roaring rapids, which sent it out of control into a tree.

Six people drowned.

An eyewitness painted a picture of the cataclysm in a newspaper account from the *Sydney Morning Herald*: "As night drew in the unavailing cries for assistance all around became fearfully harassing. Crash after crash announced the fall of some house and the screams that followed the engulphing (sic) of those who clung till the water reached its greatest height, about 11 o'clock at night, and began to fall at 3 A.M. on Saturday.

"Up to this time, about 34 houses had been washed away and 60 lives lost. Numbers who were carried away by the stream saved themselves by clinging to trees."

This is where Yarri, a Waridjuri shepherd, entered the picture. Setting out in a bark canoe he had carved himself, he navigated the raging waters through the darkness to the nearly submerged homes. He urged settlers stranded on the roofs of their dwellings to get into the canoe, then ferried them to the safety of the riverbank. Another Waridjuri man, Jackey, joined him.

Only one passenger could fit in the canoe at a time, so it took them several trips to effect the rescue of 49 people. Among them was innkeeper John Spencer, whose relative had sought to hire out his boat before its fatal accident. He spent a day and a half in a tree, naked except for a cashbox around his neck, before Yarri rescued him.

Others were not so fortunate. A hundred people are estimated to have died in the flood, which has been called the worst natural disaster in the nation's history. The waters rose so high that horses and cattle were reportedly found wedged in tree branches when the river receded the next day. Only one building, the flour mill on Morley's Creek, survived the flood intact.

Everything else was gone.

For his trouble, Yarri received an engraved brass breastplate and eventually had a bridge named after him. A memorial plaque was also dedicated in his honor.

But most seem to have forgotten his bravery.

"Considering the situation for aborigines at the time did not evoke generosity towards white settlers, Yarri's efforts were truly remarkable," New South Wales Premier Nick Greiner said in unveiling the plaque in 1990.

Indeed, the mistreatment Yarri received in his later years from the visitors to Gundagai, described at the outset of this chapter, was hardly unusual. Not only did the settlers bring with them foreign disease that ravaged the Aboriginal population, they confiscated their land (justifying their actions by saying that the indigenous people did not fence their land) and adopted policies that institutionalized the discrimination against them.

By the 1920s, the indigenous population of Australia had fallen from as many as 750,000 at the time the first settlers arrived to as few as 50,000. Indigenous laborers often went without pay, while the colonists and their descendants sought to systematically exterminate the Aboriginal culture. Indigenous families often were forced to give up their children, who were raised by citizens of European descent, in an attempt at forced assimilation.

The aborigines themselves were long denied citizenship, and until 1965 — nearly two centuries after the settlers' arrival — they were not allowed to vote in state and federal elections.

Is it any wonder, in light of all this, that Yarri's heroic actions were forgotten by so many?

But, fortunately, not by all.

"In memory of Yarri, hero of Gundagai. An Aboriginal man who rescued 49 people on the night of the 24th of June, 1852 from the flooded Murrumbidgee River in Gundagai rests here."

— Yarri's headstone

Karen Klein
Bullied on the Bus

When Karen Klein got on the bus in Greece, N.Y., during the summer of 2012, she was just trying to help kids. She had eight grandkids of her own. She was a widow, and her son had committed suicide ten years earlier.

But the middle school students on the bus that day didn't want to help her. They wanted to tease her. They repeatedly poked and taunted the 68-year-old grandmother. "My knife would go through you like butter, because it's all … lard," one said. A student even threatened to break into her house and have a pit bull attack her. They called her fat. They called her a troll. And worse.

When she started to cry, they teased her even more.

"Are you sweating? Karen, Karen! Are you sweating?" one asked.

"I'm crying," she said.

When a videotape of the harassment was posted online, viewers were outraged. It went viral, getting more than a million views on YouTube and attracting attention from the mainstream media, as well. One person who saw the video, a Canadian named Max Sidorov, started a campaign to raise $5,000 so she could take a nice vacation. The response overwhelming: In the end, more than 32,000 people donated over $700,000. The money allowed Klein to pay off her house and her car… and do one more thing. She used $100,000 to start her own anti-bullying foundation.

"The goal of the anti-bullying campaign is to help teach kids and teens about being kind, friendly and playing nice with others," Klein said. "Because of my own personal bullying story, I've now decided to become an advocate for change."

The Karen Klein Anti-Bullying Foundation has identified four goals. One is to provide anti-bullying counseling services in schools around the world. Another is to create an educational curriculum that addresses the issue of bullying. Klein also hopes to support other organizations and develop media programs that will raise an awareness of bullying.

"If we were able to raise $700,000 or one person (me), I am sure we can raise thousands more for kids who are bullied every day," Klein wrote on the foundation's website.

Sidorov also started a foundation, called Seven Million Acts of Love, which provides free counseling to victims, as well as to bullies and families affected by bullying. An associated project, Love is Moving, was created to spotlight good deeds performed by youths.

As for the seventh-graders who tormented Klein, some were given yearlong suspensions from the school, and many wrote letters of apology. Four wound up going to an alternative school and were assigned 50 hours of community service at a nursing home.

Klein herself says she's never been able to watch the video of her abuse that started it all. "I just couldn't," she said. "I hope nobody else has to go through anything like that. ... It's not right. How would you like it if somebody did it to you?"

"I'm afraid some of the kids have been bullied, and that's why they did what they did."

— Karen Klein

Claudette Colvin
Bullied on the Bus II

Karen Klein wasn't the first person to be bullied on a bus. But she is in good company.

The best-known story is that of Rosa Parks, who refused a bus driver's order to relinquish her seat in the "colored" section of the vehicle to a white passenger once the white section was filled. The year was 1955, when separate and unequal was still the rule of thumb in Montgomery, Ala. — where Parks lived — and across much of the South.

But there is something more to the story. This wasn't Parks' first run-in with the bus driver, one James F. Blake. Twelve years earlier, she had paid her fare and boarded a bus when Blake told her she had violated city rules by coming in through the *front* door. She could ride the bus, he told her, but she'd have to get off and enter again through the rear door.

Parks complied, only to watch as the driver pulled away and left her standing in the rain before she had a chance to get back on.

The next time she saw him, he was asking her and three other passengers to give up their seats in deference to a white man. She didn't realize at the time that Blake was the same man who had left her standing in the rain more than a decade earlier, but she did realize his request — or rather demand — was offensive.

Four blacks would have to give up their seats because it was against the rules to allow any African-Americans to sit in the same row with white riders.

First two women across the aisle moved. Then the man sitting in the window seat next to Parks rose. She shifted to let him out, then moved to where he had been sitting.

"The driver wanted us to stand up, the four of us," she remembered. "We didn't move at the beginning, but he says, 'Let me have those seats.' And the other three people moved, but I didn't."

Blake asked her again, "Are you going to stand up?"

"No," Parks responded. "I'm tired of being treated like a second-class-citizen."

"I'm going to have you arrested."

"You can do that."

Blake parked the bus in front of a local theater and called his supervisor. A few minutes later, police arrived to arrest Parks, who was ultimately found guilty and had to pay a $10 fine, plus $4 in court costs. On the day of her trial, however, the Women's Political Council — a civil rights organization formed a decade earlier in Montgomery — distributed thousands of leaflets calling for blacks to boycott the bus service on Monday in protest.

Some 40,000 African-Americans did exactly that. They rode in black-owned cabs. They carpooled. Many of them walked. The effort was so successful that organizers formed a new group to extend the effort, electing Martin Luther King as their president. The boycott stretched on for weeks, then months, then more than a year.

King would later write that "Mrs. Parks was ideal for the role assigned to her by history," calling her "one of the most respected people in the Negro community."

The arrest of Rosa Parks, however, was not the case that ultimately ended racial segregation on public buses. Instead, it was a separate incident nine months earlier that became the catalyst for change in Montgomery and across the United States. It involved a

15-year-old girl named Claudette Colvin who, like Parks, was arrested for refusing to give up her seat.

Colvin, a student at Booker T. Washington High School, refused a driver's order to yield her seat when a white woman got on the bus. Protesting that her constitutional rights were being violated, Colvin was handcuffed, arrested and removed by force from the bus.

Though Colvin had "had years of bad experiences of segregation," she said her protest was a spur-of-the moment act. "I think that when you have a gut feeling that something is not right and is unfair, that you should speak out," she said. "If you feel strongly enough, stand up alone if you have to stand up alone."

For taking a stand, she was rewarded with ridicule. She noticed some of the teachers at her school seemed uncomfortable around her, and so were some of her friends' parents. Perhaps, she thought, they were embarrassed that a teenager had taken a stand when they had failed to do so.

She had gone out on a limb, and now she felt abandoned.

"When I got back to school, more and more students turned against me," she recalled. "Everywhere I went, people pointed at me and whispered. Some kids would snicker when they saw me coming down the hall. ... I hadn't expected to become a hero, but I sure didn't expect this."

It took Parks' action nine months later to galvanize the community and, eventually, Colvin's case was the one chosen to test the Jim Crow laws that had victimized her and Parks in much the same way.

Colvin and three other women became plaintiffs in the case called *Browder v. Gayle* that wound its way through the court system. Browder was one of the other three plaintiffs, a homemaker from Montgomery. Gayle was W.A. Gayle, the mayor of Montgomery, who had listened to concerns from the Women's Political Council a year before the Colvin incident and had chosen to do nothing.

It wasn't as though their concerns had been unreasonable. They had called for an end to the practice of forcing black passengers to stand when empty seats were available, the requirement that they enter through the rear doors of a bus, and bus drivers' refusal to stop at every street corner in black neighborhoods (something that was done in white areas).

Several months into the boycott, a district court ruled in the Browder case. "The enforced segregation of black and white passengers on motor buses operating in the City of Montgomery violates the Constitution and laws of the United States," specifically the Fourteenth Amendment, it ruled.

The Supreme Court later affirmed this decision.

"Whatever my individual desires were to be free, I was not alone," Parks said. "There were many others who felt the same way."

"When it comes to justice, there is no easy way to get it. You can't sugarcoat it. You have to take a stand and say, 'This is not right.'"

— Claudette Colvin

Jackie Robinson
Bullied on the Bus III

The decision in *Browder v. Gayle* must have gratified yet another individual who had been harassed on a bus several years earlier — a man who is perhaps more famous even than Rosa Parks, but whose story of discrimination in the military has been largely forgotten. Unlike the incidents involving Parks and Karen Klein, his actions didn't generate much publicity, in part because the incident occurred on an Army base just outside Waco, Texas.

The young lieutenant named Jackie Robinson was riding on a bus there, sitting next to another officer's wife — who was African-American but light skinned — when the driver told him he'd have to move to a seat nearer the back of the bus.

Robinson refused.

He had been forced to jump through hoops just to get to officer school in the first place, even though the Army's admissions policy was supposed to be colorblind. It had taken the intervention of boxing champ Joe Louis — whom Robinson had befriended and who, in turn, had connections in the War Department — to break the racist logjam that had kept their applications from being approved in the first place.

Now Robinson was a lieutenant. And here he was in camp, being told that he would have to move to the back of the bus for the same reason Rosa Parks and Claudette Colvin would be told to move several years later in Montgomery: African-Americans were not allowed to sit in the same row as white people. Those were the rules.

Robinson was not about to move. But the bus driver wasn't backing down, either. Once the bus had reached Robinson's stop, he pressed his argument, now joined by the dispatcher, Beverly Younger, who referred to Robinson using the N-word. Several military police officers arrived and suggested that Robinson accompany them to police headquarters. But when they got there, another MP ran up to meet them and asked if the lieutenant was on board ... punctuating his question with another instance of the N-word.

The indignity of this racist epithet, now used a second time, infuriated Robinson, and he threatened to "break in two" anyone, regardless of rank, who used it.

His reaction would prove costly: Robinson was subsequently court-martialed, accused of failing to obey a direct command and showing disrespect toward a superior officer. (Interestingly, as a lieutenant, Robinson outranked the MPs who initially came to confront him.)

But like Rosa Parks years later, he wouldn't allow himself to be railroaded. Confined to quarters, he wrote to the NAACP and to Truman Gibson, aide to the secretary of war. It was Gibson who had intervened at Joe Louis' request on behalf of Robinson and other black athletes being kept out of officer candidates' school.

Gibson told him to sit tight, as no action could be taken before the trial, but also asked to be kept informed about the proceedings.

It proved to be sound advice.

At trial, the prosecution's case against Robinson fell apart. A former commanding officer called to testify said he had specifically sought to have Robinson assigned to his battalion, repeatedly using the word "excellent" in describing the lieutenant's attitude and performance.

One prosecution witness denied using the N-word, but his testimony was contradicted by another MP who declared that he had done so. Then there was the question of Robinson's refusal to obey a direct order supposedly issued by Capt. Gerald Bear, the assistant provost marshal. Under questioning, however, Bear admitted he couldn't say whether he'd ever actually issued any orders to Robinson.

In the end, the lieutenant was acquitted of all charges and wound up receiving an honorable discharge.

That was the end of it.

Unfortunately, it wasn't the end of people being taunted, bullied and displaced after taking their seats on a bus. Claudette Colvin, Rosa Parks and Karen Klein are proof enough of that. But they're also proof of something else: bullies don't always win. Character, resolve and principle still count for a quite a bit.

And change is possible.

50 UNDEFEATED

"I'm not concerned with your liking or disliking me. ... All I ask is that you respect me as a human being."

— Jackie Robinson

Carrie Buck
Bucking the System

Carrie Buck was slow. At least that's what they said at the time. That's how they justified what they did to her. She was just 17 years old at the time, but her genetics were flawed.

So they said.

Her mother, Emma, had been placed in an asylum for the "epileptic and feebleminded," and the people in charge of this venerable institution decreed that Carrie was sure to follow in her mother's footsteps. According to them, she was covered under a state law that prescribed a specific treatment for a "probable potential parent of socially inadequate offspring."

Such a woman was to be sterilized — and Carrie Buck, they said, was such a woman.

The fight was on.

The case eventually wound up before the U.S. Supreme Court, which took the case in 1927.

Albert Priddy, superintendent of the Virginia Colony for the Epileptic and Feebleminded testified that Emma Buck had "a record of immorality, prostitution, untruthfulness and syphilis." Further, he said of the entire Buck family: "These people belong to the shiftless, ignorant and worthless class of anti-social whites of the South."

The sins of the fathers — and the mothers — were definitely being attributed to Carrie Buck. Or, more accurately, the prejudices against them. A man named Harry Laughlin, who had never met

Buck accused her in a written deposition of "moral delinquency" and "feeblemindedness."

Laughlin had his own agenda. He was a champion of eugenics, the practice of ensuring that good genes (as the name suggests) would be passed on to future generations ... by weeding out the bad genes. An important weapon in their arsenal: forced sterilization of would-be parents who were deemed somehow unsuitable or deficient.

If this sounds a lot like Adolf Hitler's plan to create a supposed master race, it's no coincidence. The case against Carrie Buck served as a sort of precedent for Hitler's program, which took some of its cues from Laughlin and wound up sterilizing some 350,000 people. In the University of Heidelberg in Germany awarded Laughlin an honorary degree in recognition for his work in "the science of racial cleansing." This happened in 1936, the same year sprinter Jesse Owens made a mockery of Hitler's doctrine of Aryan supremacy at the Berlin Olympics. But that's another story.

The case against Carrie Buck would have been malicious and cruel enough if she had actually been promiscuous and, as her accusers put it, feebleminded. The fact is she was neither. Yes, she had given birth to a child out of wedlock, a scandal in that day. But true scandal is the fact that her rapist, a relative of her foster parents, went free while she was committed to an asylum to cover it up.

Carrie Buck was, in fact, a woman of normal intelligence who gave birth to a daughter of normal intelligence. Her child Vivian brought home a first-grade report card that placed her on the honor roll as a "B" student and gave her an "A" for deportment. But Vivian was just a baby at the time Buck's case went to court, and what counted was the testimony of a sociologist from the Eugenics Record Office who examined the infant and concluded that she was "not quite normal" and "below average."

It didn't help Buck's case that her own lawyer was actually a member of the governing board for the institution to which she had been committed. It's hard to imagine a clearer conflict of interest. Yet the Supreme Court, led by no less a figure than Oliver Wendell Holmes, didn't seem to care about any of this. Instead, the justices voted 8-1 against Buck, with Holmes callously writing in his opinion: "It is better for all the world, if instead of waiting to execute degenerate offspring for crime, or to let them starve for their imbecility, society can prevent those who are manifestly unfit from continuing their kind."

The only dissenting justice did not write an opinion.

Not only was Carrie Buck sterilized, but the ruling paved the way for more than 8,000 Virginia residents to be suffer the same fate.

And the ramifications of the decision spread far beyond the state line. As of 1956, more than half the states (27) had sterilization laws on the books. California sterilized more than 20,000 people in the cause of "race betterment," more than any other state and nearly a third of the nation's total. Ulysses S. Webb, who served as the state's attorney general from 1902 to 1939, advocated sterilization for "inebriates, prostitutes, tramps, and habitual paupers found in our county poor-asylums."

In North Carolina, forced sterilization continued until 1974 and affected some 7,600 people. Among them was Elaine Riddick, who was sterilized at the age of 14 after being raped and giving birth to a son in 1968, nearly half a century after the Buck case.

In 2012, state lawmakers in North Carolina's lower house approved a plan to pay each surviving victim of forced sterilization $50,000 in compensation, but the idea ran aground in the state Senate over concerns about its cost.

Still, Riddick said she planned to continue the fight — the same fight Buck had waged decades earlier. "I have given North Carolina a chance to justify what they had wronged," she said in announcing her intention to pursue legal action. "I gave them until the last moment, but now I have no other choice. These people here don't care about these victims. I will die before I let them get away with this."

They did get away with it in Carrie Buck's case, and she did eventually die without seeing any compensation. Adding to her tragedy was the death of her only child, Vivian, from an intestinal illness a year after she made the honor roll.

In spite of it all, Carrie Buck persevered. She was paroled from Virginia Colony shortly after she was sterilized and eventually wed William Eagle; they remained married for a quarter-century until his passing. Hardly promiscuous by any standard. She became an avid reader and, to all accounts, was a woman of normal intelligence.

She lived a long, full life, and her main regret was that she was never able to have more children.

"Three generations of imbeciles are enough."

— Oliver Wendell Holmes

Crystal Vera
Real Royalty

Crystal Vera and Cinthia Covarrubias didn't know each other, but they had a couple of things in common. Both attended high school in Fresno, California, and each wanted to be involved in their respective schools' homecoming festivities.

Covarrubias wanted to be prom king at Fresno High, and Vera wanted to be prom queen at Roosevelt, just a few miles away.

The year was 2007. When Covarrubias, who had been born female but who identified as a transgender individual, was nominated, the school tried to put her in the queen category. It was against district policy for her to run for king. But she held her ground.

"I would never have run for anything if I had to wear a dress," she said. "My freshman year, I started feeling different. When I decided to change to be like this, all of a sudden I said, 'Wow, I feel OK. I feel like finally, I'm being me.' "

District officials eventually altered their policy after their lawyers advised them that a California law passed seven years earlier protected students' rights to be open about their gender identity at school. In the end, Covarrubias donned a tuxedo and competed against six boys vying for the honor of homecoming king. She didn't win, but she is believed to have been the first transgender student to compete openly for a spot on the prom court.

"Cinthia finished her recent transition to dress and look how she felt most comfortable. She was so happy and comfortable with herself," said Tiffani Sanchez, Fresno High's Gay-Straight Alliance advisor. "She came out of her shell and just blossomed. I had never seen her so happy and outgoing before. I can think of no other word to describe it besides true liberation."

Covarrubias' experience inspired Vera to follow in her footsteps. And the Roosevelt High student ended up taking it one step further — by winning. Vera, whose birth name was Johnny and stood 6 foot, 4 inches tall in heels and a flowing pink dress, won her crown with five out of every six votes cast.

"For me, it's about more than a crown," Vera told *The Fresno Bee*. "It's about me saying to people, 'Come out and be who you want to be.'"

Vera's courage and leadership were already in evidence at Roosevelt before the prom. She had served as class vice president and was a member of the cheerleading squad. She had actually been a prince in a previous homecoming court. Intent on succeeding, she repeated inspirational sayings every day as she walked to school.

"There were all those statistics about transgender kids committing suicide," she told *The Bee*. "People would look at me and say I was going to do drugs or be a prostitute, and I would just tell myself, 'I'm not going to let anyone but me tell me what I'm going to be.'"

"It's just so wonderful to know that times are changing. People are changing. Things like this bring us hope as individuals that things will be better off for us."

— Crystal Vera

John Amagoalik
High Arctic Exile

Many people think of Canada as a nation of two cultures. In the east, there's the province of Quebec, where French is the dominant language and the largest city — Montreal — has very much the flavor of an Old World city. To the west lie the English-speaking provinces, stretching all the way to the Pacific and the province of British Columbia, whose very name continues the imperial legacy of the United Kingdom.

To the north?

The Aurora Borealis, a few polar bears and frozen tundra — as John Amagoalik put it, a "wasteland where nobody lives."

But Amagoalik knew better, and he also knew that there were more than two cultures holding Canada together. There was also a third — the Inuit culture, which made the Old World character of Montreal seem positively novel by comparison.

When he was 5 years old, Amagoalik and his family were one of several relocated from an old fur-trading post in northern Quebec about 1,200 miles to the north as part of the High Arctic relocation project. This took place shortly after the start of the Cold War, when Canada was eager to establish sovereignty over the region by using these few Inuit families as "human flagpoles" to discourage any possible Soviet or U.S. claims to the region. There were fewer than a hundred of them, hardly enough to establish a workable community

— especially when the families were deposited at two or three separate locations.

"We were still on the ship when we were told that one group had to get off at the next destination and the other half would go to another site," Amagoalik recalls.

There, they were abandoned, left without sufficient food or the supplies necessary to make clothing or even tent shelters. In their new "home," sunlight or darkness could last for almost the entire day, depending on the season. They were hit by blizzards in the middle of summer and temperatures of 50 below in winter. Hunting was difficult in the pitch black of a daylong night, and even harder because the muskox, like the Inuit themselves, were emaciated from hunger.

"Even if there were healthy muskox that we could find, we were informed by the (Royal Canadian Mounted Police) that this was an endangered species and it was under protection by international law, and we couldn't harvest them," Amagoalik said.

He recalled scenes from his childhood of sick and hungry adults who pleaded with officials from the Mounties to let them return home.

To no avail.

They had been told that, if their new home was not to their liking, they could return after a year. But this offer was subsequently withdrawn, and the government forced them to stay put. Not only were they left stranded far from the life they had once known, they were dehumanized as well — issued nameless leather ID tags stamped with numbers and the words "Eskimo Identification Canada" inside an outline of the British crown.

Despite the hardships they were forced to endure, they persevered and managed to make a home for themselves alongside caribou, arctic wolves, muskoxen, arctic hares and lemmings in a harsh land that provided them with few necessities and even fewer comforts. They learned the migration routes of the beluga whales, and they began to hunt the great mammals, which helped to ensure their survival.

In 1976, discussions began on the possibility of carving out a section of the Northwest Territories as an Inuit territory. Six years later, a majority of residents in the Northwest Territories approved of the idea, and in 1999, Nunavut Territory was established by the Canadian Parliament.

Amagoalik was instrumental in the effort to make this happen — so much so that he is often called the "Father of Nunavut." Having served as regional information officer for the Northwest Territories and co-chair of the Inuit Committee on National Issues, he spent six years as chief commissioner of the Nunavut Implementation Committee, until Nunavut Territory was finally established a few months before the start of a new millennium.

Today, Nunavut is thriving. It encompasses a three-quarters of a million square miles, making it larger than all but 14 nations of the world. "It's a bit mind-boggling," Amagoalik said when the deal was first struck. "This agreement will make the Inuit of Nunavut the largest landholders in North America."

The territory is, in fact, twice the size of Alaska.

Its population, by contrast, is small but growing rapidly, with the territorial capital of Iqaluit on Baffin Island boasting more than 6,000 residents in 2006 — an 18 percent increase in just five years. Four out of every five residents in Nunavut are Inuit, and two-thirds of the territorial population speaks Inuktitut, the language of the Inuit.

It took until 2010, but the Canadian government finally apologized for its treatment of the Inuit forced to relocate more than a half-century earlier.

"We're apologizing for promises that were made and not kept," said John Duncan, minister of northern and Indian affairs. "Despite the suffering and hardship, the relocatees and their descendants were successful in building vibrant communities. … The government of Canada recognizes that these communities have contributed to a strong Canadian presence in the High Arctic."

"Finally, we will have a government that will speak our language, know our history, share our priorities."

— John Amagoalik

STEPHEN H. PROVOST

Linah Kilimo
The Unkindest Cut

In 2011, the Kenyan Parliament outlawed a barbaric practice that — just a few years earlier — had been a requirement for membership on that same body.

Linah Jebii Kilimo knew about that requirement all too well.

If you were a woman, you had to be circumcised. That was the polite term for it, but the procedure itself was anything but polite. More accurately, it was known as female genital mutilation, and it was — or rather is — practiced across a broad swath of Africa. An estimated 92 million females on the continent have been subjected to the operation, many on the assumption that it will inhibit their desire to have sex.

Kilimo was fortunate. Or, rather, she made her own good fortune. She ran away from home to avoid the torture and indignity of having her genitals cut. Yet far from being rewarded for her courage, she instead became the object of a different sort of indignity: Kilimo found herself shunned and ridiculed as one outside the norms of society.

"People turned their faces away, as if I smelled, as I passed by," she said. "Even as a grown woman, because I had no undergone FGM, they treated me as a child."

When she ran for a seat in Parliament in 2002, her opponents charged that she was not fit to hold office. Fortunately, she had an ace in the hole. There was a myth in Kenyan folklore that warring parties who wished to end their conflict should send an uncircumcised girl to make peace between them. Using this as an argument in her favor, she was able to win the election and, upon taking office, immediately set about working to ban mutilation. It was a daunting task. The practice has been deeply ingrained in Kenyan society, practiced by 38 of its 43 ethnic groups, and was particularly entrenched among some communities. The practice was ubiquitous in the Maasai, Somali, Pokot, Kisii, Kuria and Samburu cultures.

Among the Kisii, the rate was 96 percent.

Shortly before the new law was passed, a 14-year-old girl named Ruth expressed resentment at her forced mutilation. "When people see me and I smile at them, they think I like what I went through," she said. "But I wish I could run away. My grandmother says I must be cut so I can be a good girl in the future."

Despite her opposition, her father was adamant than she undergo the procedure: "As a man, you want to bring up your child in the way of your people, and for us, being circumcised is one of them," he said. "She will be a good woman to her husband in the future. When people say we should stop what we have done all along, I just laugh."

To Ruth and others forced to go through the procedure, however, it was far from a laughing matter. More than a crime against the female body, it was a symbol of discrimination and repression that was keeping women from realizing their full potential. Kilimo put it this way: "Before the cut, you are safe; after the cut, your future is gone with the wind."

And no, it isn't true that unmutilated women forfeit the chance of ever being married. Kilimo herself married a government engineer, and together they have five children.

"The government can only tackle poverty and illiteracy in the pastoral region when FGM is banned, since it is the root cause of illiteracy and economic woes of these communities," Kilimo argued in support of the bill to outlaw mutilation. Her best argument, however, was the sheer brutality of the practice. Sometimes, it involved the act of puncturing the clitoris; in extreme cases, it meant slicing off the entire clitoris along with the labia and sewing the cavity virtually shut, leaving only a tiny opening to allow for the passage of urine and blood.

"We forced the male parliamentarians to watch movies that depicted female genital mutilation — what it looks like in real life," Kilimo said. "They could not bear to see it."

The bill that passed the Kenyan Parliament not only made mutilation illegal, it had teeth. Anyone found guilty of the engaging in the practice — or hiring someone else to do so — faces three to seven years behind bars and a fine of nearly $6,000. Anyone who causes a death while performing the procedure can be sentenced to life in prison.

"Today is a great day," Kilimo said when the law was passed. "Parliament has protected the girl child from the monster that is FGM. This will mark a rise in retention and completion rates in schools."

The struggle, however, is far from over. Mutilation remains widespread in several African countries that have banned it. Foremost among these is Egypt, where more than 9 in 10 women have been affected. In Kenya, too, it is one thing to pass a law (even one that includes stringent penalties) and quite another to enforce it in the face of a stubborn tradition that has for decades defied attempts by women, reformers, religious leaders to end it.

Though the practice isn't as common in Kenya as it is in Egypt, it is still difficult to root out. A law against mutilation known as the Children's Act was adopted a decade before the most recent measure, yet it was largely ineffective at curtailing the practice.

The attitude of 14-year-old Ruth's father remains common.

After the Children's Act passed, those who practiced mutilation "resorted to more secretive ways of doing it," said Pamela Mbuvi, children's officer for the Kisii District. "We have caught a few people doing it and at least five have been jailed that I know of, but the secrecy that the perpetrators use makes it hard to effectively use the law to end the practice."

The new law closed many of the legal loopholes left in place under the Children's Act. Meanwhile, attempts to marginalize the practice are having an effect, and the efforts of people like Kilimo are bearing fruit — efforts that support legal remedies with education, a key element of Kilimo's drive for reform.

"Laws targeting specifically FGM are an important step in ending the practice, but the law alone cannot do it because it is a traditional practice and is deeply rooted," she said. "Remember, people who strongly believe in culture are at times ready to die for it. My suggestion is, let the government and anybody working for children's rights carry out education and awareness among the community to let them know the dangers (of mutilation). Those campaigns have been carried out, but they must be continuous."

Along these lines, the signs are encouraging. One group began training 31 primary school teachers to educate students and parents alike about preventing mutilation. Another organization seeks to encourage alternative rites of passage for young women.

In 2011, a total of 15 communities within Kenya announced a commitment to ending mutilation. Among them were the Pokot and Chamus groups, where the practice had been especially common. One group of young Chamus men pledged in public that they would marry unmutilated girls.

Said Kilimo: "The girls can now concentrate on their education without being forced to engage in the outdated cultural practice."

"Female genital mutilation puts those who undergo it through a lot of physical and psychological pain, and they need support."

— Linah Kilimo

Hank
One Great Dane

Each year, between 3 and 4 million walk through those doors and never come back out.

That's not exactly right. Some have to be carried.

They die, the vast majority of them, within a few days from a "humane" lethal injection — not too different from the kind that convicted killers have challenged repeatedly as cruel and unusual punishment. Yet the punishment these cats and dogs receive is anything but unusual, and unlike a murderer on death row, they haven't done anything to deserve it.

Too often, they've been victims of abuse themselves.

Take Hank, for example, a 2-year-old Great Dane and companion of a Kansas City woman called McKenzie. Hank wasn't facing a death sentence at a shelter, but he nearly lost his life defending McKenzie from an attack that could have killed them both.

Like so many animals in shelters across the country, Hank hadn't done anything wrong. But that didn't matter to the man who hit him repeatedly with a hammer in a beating that endangered his life — and which, if he hadn't been present, would likely have cost McKenzie hers.

It came at the hand of 30-year-old McKenzie's abusive boyfriend, who one day threw her through a wall, then picked up a hammer and assaulted her. "When my Great Dane ... heard me scream," she later recalled, he laid on top of me. I tried to get him out of the way, but he received many blows from my abuser."

He kicked Hank in the hips.

He punched him.

Then, when Hank went after the man, he beat him some more and threw him off the porch by the neck.

"He drug him from our house a block to a very busy street and let him go in the middle of the street while cars were coming," McKenzie recalled. "And he said if I reached for him or called for him, he would shoot him where he stood."

So instead, she ran.

She got to the car and saw her attacker pointing a shotgun at her head, but she was able to get away. Because Hank had shielded her, she was uninjured and was able to find police, who arrested her attacker. When they took her back home, Hank was lying next to the house, badly hurt.

The 110-pound dog was taken to a veterinarian and treated for broken ribs and a broken hip.

But that's not the end of the story.

Police advised McKenzie (whose actual name was withheld due to her status as an abuse victim) to consider staying at a women's shelter and gave her the number of the Rose Brooks Center, a women's shelter. When she called, however, she was told she was welcome to stay there — but she'd have to find somewhere else for Hank. The center accepted women and welcomed children, too, but it simply had no place for pets.

McKenzie, it seemed, was out of luck. But she wasn't about to leave Hank out on the street or take him to an animal shelter. "He's my angel," she told a volunteer advocate. "We'll just sleep in the car."

As it turned out, however, she didn't have to. The center, decided to bend the rules — and more.

It seems McKenzie's situation was far from unique.

"Over the years, our crisis hotline has received countless calls from women who desire to leave their abuser, but ultimately decide to remain in a dangerous home because they fear their abuser will injure or even kill their beloved dog or can," said Susan Miller, CEO of the Rose Brooks Center. "Abusers threaten and injure pets in order to control their victims and to create an environment of fear within the home."

Indeed, Miller said, more than 8 in 10 women in domestic violence shelters say their abusers also abused their pets. And 4 in 10 refuse to leave their abusers because of it.

In response, the shelter broke ground on a new wing designed to include a shelter with seven kennels — not the kind where pets are euthanized, but a haven for them to stay near their human companions while they both heal.

As for Hank, the Humane Society of the United States honored him as the fifth annual Valor Dog of the Year.

Every day, more than 25,000 victims of domestic violence find refuge in emergency shelters or transitional housing each day. And each year, 6 out of every 10 dogs and 7 of every 10 cats taken to shelters and human societies every year are killed. With a single act of loyalty and courage, Hank provided the sort of inspiration that can make a difference to them both.

"No matter if it's two-legged or four-legged, it's that bond of love. There's nothing more healing than that."

— McKenzie

Kathy Kusner

Not Just Horsing Around

Kathy Kusner had ridden in the Olympics. She'd been riding since she was ten years old.

Three years after that first Olympic appearance in dressage, she applied for a jockey license in Maryland. Approval should have been a no-brainer. But the year was 1967, and many people thought women had no business competing against men — no matter how good they were.

Kusner's application was denied. The Maryland Racing Commission complained that she "bounced in the saddle" and failed to radiate an "impression of strength and authority" when she rode. And its chairman told *Sports Illustrated* magazine that Kusner was "an able rider in many respects, but if she were allowed to ride in regular races ... who'd be to blame if she got hurt?"

Kusner wasn't worried.

"Horse riding is more is more a game of technique and skill than strength," she told reporters. "It's the same as playing chess with men, so I don't intend to give up the fight."

She didn't, and in the end, she won.

A year after the racing commission turned her down, a judge ordered the panel to license her, ruling that its failure to do so had been sex discrimination.

Kusner opened the door to other women who became jockeys, but the process was slow. Barbara Jo Rubin eventually became the first woman to win a thoroughbred racing event. Rubin had been struck by polio as a child and got into riding as a form of therapy to strengthen her legs — a heavy dose of irony considering Kusner had been denied a license to ride because she supposedly wasn't strong enough.

Sexism, however, was obviously still alive and well. Rubin even had her trailer stoned on one occasion.

It was on Feb. 22, 1969 that Rubin became the first woman to enter the winner's circle at a recognized track — at Charles Town Races in West Virginia. In fact, she ended up winning 11 of her first 22 races. A year and a half later, Diane Crump became the first woman to ride in the Kentucky Derby. But it wasn't until 1993 that Julie Krone became the first woman to win a Triple Crown race, when she rode Colonial Affair to victory in the Belmont Stakes.

And Kathy Kusner?

She returned to the Olympics in 1972 and won a silver medal in the dressage. She rode races all over the world, becoming the first licensed jockey in Chile, Colombia, Germany, Mexico, Panama, Peru and South Africa. Kusner eventually retired as a jockey, but she was hardly finished. She went on to become one of the first women to pilot a Learjet for the world's largest charter jet company, Executive Jet Aviation. She has been scuba diving all over the world.

That's not all. Kusner has competed frequently in distance running, having won the Colorado Pike's Peak Ultra-Marathon three times in her age bracket. In all, Kusner has competed in more than 100 marathons and more than 60 ultra-marathons.

And the Maryland Racing Commission questioned her strength. That's a good one.

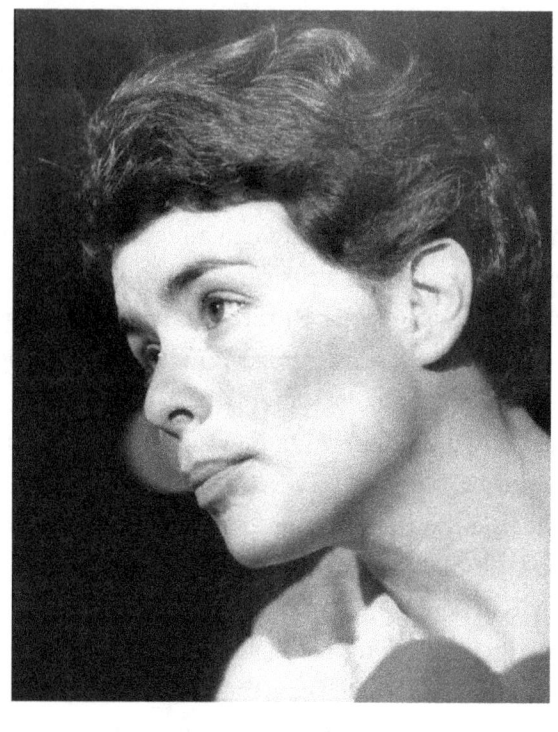

*"I don't care about proving anything at all.
I just want to ride horses."*

— Kathy Kusner

Roberta Stewart
Set in Stone

By any measure, the Taliban regime that rose to power in Afghanistan during the last decade of the 20th century was brutally oppressive.

Colleges were closed to women, and they were removed from most segments of the workforce. Members of the minority Hazara ethnic group were targeted for oppression and slaughter — one incident of ethnic cleansing reportedly left as many as 6,000 Hazara dead, some of whom had been left to suffocate inside locked containers.

Then there were the statues. A year into the new millennium, Taliban leader Mullah Omar decreed that all statues in Afghanistan be destroyed. This order extended to the Buddha statues of Bamiyan, a pair of gigantic figures that had been carved into the side of sandstone cliffs nearly 1,500 years earlier.

The Taliban dynamited them, reducing them to dust.

This isn't a story of Taliban atrocities. But it does deal with religious freedom, a soldier who fought in Afghanistan and a sacred symbol that serves as a monument.

Sgt. Patrick Stewart was born in Reno, Nevada, and enlisted in the U.S. Army shortly after graduating from Washoe High School in 1989. A decorated soldier, he served in Kuwait and Korea before being discharged from the Army in 1996. He returned to duty as a member of the National Guard, assigned to Afghanistan with the 113th Aviation Regiment.

Stewart was 35 years old when a rocket-propelled grenade struck his helicopter as he was returning to base in Afghanistan for refueling. He lost his life when it went down southwest of Deh Chopan, leaving behind a wife he had married only two years earlier, along with a son, a stepdaughter and a simple request: that the symbol of his faith be displayed at the Northern Nevada Veterans Memorial Cemetery, some 35 miles from where he was born.

It shouldn't have been too much to ask. The five-pointed star he sought as a memorial is the same symbol that appears fifty times on the American flag. It's also the same symbol that hangs from the ribbon he was awarded posthumously for heroism in combat — the Bronze Star.

In this case, however, the star would be inscribed inside a circle to remind visitors of Stewart's faith.

He was Wiccan.

And therein lay the problem — the symbol of this particular faith had not been approved for inclusion on service members' memorial plaques. A space was reserved for Stewart's plaque at the Northern Nevada cemetery, but his widow said it would remain blank until the Department of Veterans Affairs agreed to allow the symbol of his faith to be displayed there.

"It's discrimination," she told the *Las Vegas Review Journal*. "I had no idea that they would decline our veterans this right that they go to fight for. What religion we are doesn't matter. It's like denying who my husband is."

At the time of Stewart's death, the VA had approved 30-plus emblems of belief for inclusion on headstones and grave markers, including several variations on the cross for various Christian denominations, the Star of David, the Muslim crescent and star, as well as emblems of the Baha'i faith, Eckankar and atheism.

But Roberta Stewart, like her late husband, thought it was important to fight for what she believed in.

Her daughter, 12 years old at the time, even wrote a letter to the secretary of Veterans Affairs. "Why won't you put my dad's religion sign on a plaque?" she asked. "He respected you and your rules and went and fought for our country and died for our country …"

Stewart eventually won her battle, which was joined by several other Wiccans — followers of a nature-based faith whose creed includes an injunction to "harm none" and which includes elements of traditional witchcraft. The VA agreed in April of 2007 to expand the list of symbols acceptable for placement on veterans' memorial markers, although it did so in part "to spare taxpayers the expense of further litigation."

If the decision seemed grudging, it must have seemed even more so later in the year, when then-President George W. Bush traveled to Nevada to meet with the families of fallen veterans. Patrick Stewart's parents were invited to the gathering, as were his brother and the relatives of others from Nevada who had died in combat. Roberta Stewart's name, however, was noticeably absent from the guest list.

It shouldn't have been surprising.

Eight years earlier, Bush had appeared on a television program and commented on the idea that Wiccan gatherings should be protected on military bases under the First Amendment: "I don't think witchcraft is a religion," he said, "and I wish the military would take another look at this and decide against it."

That would have been news to Patrick Stewart, who practiced what Bush termed a non-religion.

Fortunately, his snub — intentional or otherwise — of Roberta Stewart hasn't restrained further progress for practitioners of Wicca and other Pagan faiths. In 2010, the Air Force Academy in Colorado Springs opened a prayer circle for followers of earth-based religions, a "Stonehenge in the Rockies."

It seems only fitting that they should have a place to express their beliefs after doing battle with the Taliban, whose very mission entails the suppression of beliefs they do not share. And it seems equally appropriate that Patrick D. Stewart should be honored with a sacred marker that expresses his faith.

After all, he was fighting a regime that destroyed those sacred stone carvings etched into the hills at Bamiyan.

"I feel very strongly that my husband fought for the Constitution of the United States, he was proud of his spirituality and of being a Wiccan, and he was proud to be an American."

— Roberta Stewart

Shigeru Kayano
The Forgotten People

Shigeru Kayano wouldn't budge. This land belonged to him, and it had belonged to his ancestors before him.

The Japanese government wanted to build a 10-storey dam in the Saru River, creating a huge reservoir covering roughly three square miles of forest and farmland ... not to mention a small village of thatched huts and small dwellings.

This was the home to Shigeru's people, the Ainu, the indigenous people of Hokkaido. From time immemorial, they had lived on this island — the northernmost in Japan — which rises up out of the sea from coastal plains to high mountains and volcanic vistas. The Ainu lived off the land; they hunted bear, rabbit, fox and deer, and they fished for salmon. They wore clothing made of bark or animal skins and had no written language. Light-skinned with tattoos and (on the men) long beards, they had no genetic or cultural affiliation to the modern Japanese — the Wajin. Indeed, their origins are something of a mystery, and they have been linked to bloodlines as diverse as Mongolian and Caucasian.

It was only as the Wajin began moving north across the southern island of Honshu that two groups came into contact.

And conflict.

It was a conflict the Ainu were destined to lose.

Initially, they traded with the foreigners, but the outsiders brought with them diseases such as smallpox and a thirst for wealth.

As the Ainu became more dependent upon trade with the outsiders, they gradually assumed a subservient role, similar to serfs in a feudal state. Kayano's own grandfather was among those subjugated, abducted by one of the Wajin and pressed into service aboard a fishing boat. He was able to escape, but lost a finger when it was cut off as he made his getaway.

It was around this time, in the late 19th century, that the Japanese government annexed Hokkaido to exploit its natural resources and to provide itself with a buffer against Russian imperialism. The island, they declared, was to be modernized — a step that involved a direct assault on the Ainu culture. By the turn of the century, this approach had culminated in the passage of legislation that effectively denied the Ainu status as an indigenous people. Instead, they were declared Japanese citizens and encouraged to fully assimilate into the now-dominant culture.

The Japanese government seized Ainu lands for the natural resources they coveted, then doled out a small fraction of those lands to the Ainu themselves — about five acres per family. Schools were established to immerse the Ainu in Japanese culture, but academic subjects such as science and history were not offered. Salmon fishing, meanwhile, was outlawed altogether.

"My father was arrested because he was catching salmon illegally," Kayano recalled. "I can never forget that day."

Born in 1926, Kayano lived with his family in a thatched hut with a wooden floor, where he learned the traditions of the elders. He became fluent in the Ainu tongue and learned the traditions that had been passed down orally from one generation to the next — tales of the bear and the salmon, of the *ramat* (that power possessed by all living things) and the deities known as *kamui*.

Like other Ainu villages or *kotan*, the place where Kayano was born had been built in a river basin for its proximity to the salmon run. It was called Nibutani, and like other Ainu villages, it had fallen on hard times under Japanese rule. By the early 1970s, some of its inhabitants had already left in the hope that urban life might provide greater opportunity. Those who remained were largely poor and in debt, so it wasn't a difficult decision when the government offered the families $150,000 each to surrender those five-acre plots of land it had "given" them nearly a century earlier.

For most, it was no decision at all. Economically, they had little choice ... and practically speaking, they had none at all. The government planned to take the land for its new dam whether they accepted the payment or not.

Kayano, however, decided to fight the inevitable. He refused the payment and challenged the project in court. "Can't we have one river in Hokkaido, maybe the Saru, where the salmon can spawn naturally, where crows and bears and foxes and owls — and Ainu — can be free and take the salmon to eat?" he asked. "How happy life would be."

Unfortunately, work started on the dam long before the court case was decided; by the time a ruling was issued — in favor of the government — the dam was all but completed. Yet while the case failed on one level, it succeeded on another. The Sapporo District Court affirmed that the Ainu had been present on the land prior to the arrival of the Wajin, effectively recognizing the Ainu as an indigenous population.

"The Ainu fall under the classification of a minority aboriginal race," Chief Judge Kazuo Ichimiya declared, adding that "the government should have done its utmost to consider the unique culture of the indigenous Ainu minority."

It was this indigenous status that the Japanese government had stripped from the Ainu in 1899. Now, two years shy of a century later, it was being restored. A decade after the court decision, the Japanese Diet (parliament) issued a bipartisan resolution that recognized the Ainu as "an indigenous people with a distinct language, religion and culture."

Kayano died two years before this historic resolution, yet he had in many ways paved the way for it — not only by filing the historic court case challenging the Nibutani Dam, but also as a member of the Japanese Diet itself. In 1994, he became the first Ainu elected to the legislative body, where he served for the next four years. During his tenure, he successfully pushed for passage of legislation that formally rescinded the forced-assimilation law of 1899. It also required the Japanese government to preserve and promote Ainu traditions and culture.

Kayano, however, was hardly content to leave this important task to the government. He had long ago founded the Nibutani Ainu Culture Museum, which opened in 1972 and (as of this writing) has remained open for four decades. Displayed there are Ainu folk items from Kayano's personal collection, as well as material from indigenous cultures around the world.

Still, a century of forced assimilation and economic hardship has taken its toll. In 2000, the Japanese government estimated the Ainu population at just 25,000. (By way of comparison, the Tokyo metropolitan area included more than 32 *million* residents.) Meanwhile, the Ainu language appears on the verge of disappearing entirely. Fewer than 100 individuals are said to be fluent in Ainu — a situation complicated by the fact that there is no known connection to any other language.

During his lifetime, Kayano spearheaded efforts to establish more than a dozen Ainu-language schools. He also authored scores of books on Ainu traditions and folklore, including an Ainu dictionary. He recorded and oral history of his people on compact discs. He launched an Ainu-language radio station.

"It would be a great pleasure if the children who are currently learning Ainu can be proud they learned Ainu language from me," he said.

Since his death, his son Shiro has continued his legacy. In 2012, he formed the Ainu Party with the aim of fielding candidates in 10 of the 242 races for the Diet's upper house. Though raised by an icon and a trailblazer, the younger Kayano said it was a visit to Canada, where he observed another indigenous group in the process of losing its identity, that opened his eyes to his own people's situation.

"I realized the outrageousness of one ethnicity being deprived of its own language and culture by force," he said. "I woke up to my identity as an Ainu."

So the Ainu saga continues.

The physical dam was built, but the cultural dam that has held back the Ainu people is gradually being torn down. Indeed, it is perhaps ironic to realize that, although he failed to save his land from being inundated when that dam was built, Shigeru Kayano may in fact have succeeded in helping to save something far more precious.

The Ainu culture itself.

"We want Japan to admit that Hokkaido belongs to the Ainu."

— Shigeru Kayano

Pailadzo Captanian
Going to San Francisco

Anyone with a television who has grown up in the United States during the past four decades probably knows the commercial jingle for Rice-a-Roni almost as well as "White Christmas." Sometimes, it seemed those TV ads for "the San Francisco treat" were everywhere. But if it hadn't been for a survivor of the Armenian Genocide, we never would have heard them.

In 1915, the Ottoman Empire undertook a program to exterminate the Armenian people. The Committee of Union and Progress, which had risen to power in a coup two years earlier, set its sights on Christians in general and Armenians in particular. Mehmet Nazim, a medical doctor and leading voice for the committee, declared that the Ottoman state "must be exclusively Turkish." He told a closed session of the committee that it was "absolutely necessary to eliminate the Armenian people in its entirety, so that there is no further Armenian on this earth and the very concept of Armenia is extinguished."

On April 24 of that year, 600 Armenian men were rounded up and executed in Istanbul. Some Armenian men were conscripted into the military, where they were either summarily executed or stripped of their weapons and worked beyond their physical limits until they died of exhaustion. Others were simply murdered.

Thousands of women and children were killed as well, while others were forced from their homes to be deported. Under a law passed in September, the empire was authorized to confiscate all "abandoned" property left behind by Armenians who had been deported.

Some women, evidently were given the option of remaining in their homes on the condition that they convert to Islam. "The government sent fanatical, strictly religious Muslim men and women into all the Armenian homes to spread propaganda for conversion to Islam, of course with the threat of serious consequences for those who remain in true to their beliefs," the German consul at the city of Samsun reported in the summer of 1915.

Samsun is Black Sea port on the north coast of the Anatolian peninsula, east of present-day Armenia.

Among the women living there was Pailadzo Captanian, who recalled that after the deportation was announced, a Muslim religious scholar visited her home in Samsun two or three times, encouraging her to become a Muslim.

She refused.

More than nine in 10 modern Armenians are members of the Armenian Apostolic Church, and the country was the first to adopt Christianity as its state religion — at the outset of the fourth century. It's a proud and ancient heritage. And it's therefore not surprising that few Armenians accepted the Muslim clerics' invitations to convert.

Captanian and the others who refused their offers were forcibly removed from her home and sent on what amounted to a death march through the desert to Aleppo.

During this march, they were repeatedly victimized by Ottoman police officers, or gendarmes. "What amazed me again and again was the incredible acquisitiveness of these savages," Captanian later wrote. "They were only keen of robbing, dreamed of nothing else than hidden gold. Only after they had satisfied their greed they thought of raping the women."

Some deportees, she said, resorted to hiding their valuables within their bodies — usually swallowing them and retrieving the coins when they had passed through the digestive system more than a week later.

Captanian was pregnant, but pregnant women and mothers of young children were offered no reprieve: "A woman still cringed under her labor pains when a gendarme robbed her of her clothes," she wrote. "He had not left her anything in which she could wrap her newborn that was trembling from cold."

Somehow, Captanian survived. She had had the foresight to leave her two sons in the care of a Greek family before she was deported, and she reunited with them four years later. In that same year, 1919, she wrote an account of her ordeal in French, providing the world with a powerful look at the horrors of the Armenian Genocide.

Captanian had kept a detailed diary during her journey, but it was lost, so she had to reconstruct her experiences from memory. She remembered the horrors of her journey, but she remembered other things, as well.

Among them was her own special recipe for rice pilaf.

After moving from Syria to the United States, Captanian had worked as a seamstress in New York, where she sewed curtains for President Franklin Roosevelt's home in Hyde Park. Later, when World War II was over and she had put her sons through school, she moved west to San Francisco.

She found she had some extra space, so she rented a room to Tom and Lois DeDemenico. Tom's father was an immigrant, too, and ran a pasta company in the city called Golden Grain. Lois, who was expecting their child, stayed at home with Captanian. She would later describe the experience to NPR (National Public Radio):

"I was only 18 and I was pregnant," she said. "And I had kitchen privileges. Well, I wasn't really much of a cook, and here was this Armenian lady… making yogurt on the back of the stove, all day, every day. I didn't even know what the word 'yogurt' meant."

Captanian taught the young mother-to-be how to make baklava, soup… and rice pilaf.

50 UNDEFEATED

She would improvise, using vermicelli Tom DeDemenico brought home from his father's factory, which she broke into very small pieces — the size of rice.

The DeDemenicos only lived with Captanian for four months before moving to a place of their own. But Lois remembered Captanian's recipe and served it to family members — including Ted's brother, who hit upon the idea of packaging it in a box. Because it combined rice and pasta, they called it Rice-A-Roni.

Today, some 14,000 Armenian Americans make their homes in San Francisco... Armenia is an independent nation, having declared independence from the Soviet Union on Aug. 23, 1990. More than 3 million people live there... Turkey still refuses to acknowledge that the Armenian Genocide even took place: Turkish EU Affairs Minister Egemen Bağış stated unequivocally in January of 2012 that "the 1915 incidents were not genocide."... And you can find more than 30 flavors of Rica-A-Roni available at the supermarket thanks to a woman who was courageous enough not only to endure the horrors that genocide but to chronicle its horrors for future generations.

"Is it possible to describe the horrors of such a situation? No. The ferocity of the madness that was so strong upon us is impossible to express, as it exceeds all imagination, like any human expression."

— Pailadzo Captanian

Jonathan Antoine
Singing Away the Blues

He got an apology from Simon Cowell, and that in itself is no mean feat. The critical and often sarcastic judge of various reality talent shows initially suggested that operatic singer Jonathan Antoine ditch his partner, Charlotte Jaconelli, and go solo.

The two teenage singers, who appeared on *Britain's Got Talent* — the same show that launched Susan Boyle's career — had signed up for the show as a team, and they would finish as a team. Actually, it had been Charlotte who sent in the application. "Well," Jonathan told Cowell at the time, "we came on here as a duo, and we're going to stay a duo."

It turned out to be a smart move. The pair finished second in the competition (just as Boyle had) and went on to sign a recording contract ... with Cowell's label. Its value was reported at 1 million British pounds — about $1.6 million.

Clearly, Cowell had a change of heart.

"Simon apologized to me for what he said to me in our first audition," Charlotte said. "He said, 'It's really nice to see you even though I was so mean to you before. You've improved so much since the first audition and I love you as a duo now.'"

Standing up to Cowell — who has also served as a judge on the U.S. talent shows *American Idol* and *The X Factor* — is never easy, as he can be an intimidating presence. The contestant must stand there and listen while the seated Cowell sits and passes judgment like some diabolically engineered hybrid of Roger Ebert and Pontius Pilate. Thumbs up or thumbs down … and washing his hands of the whole affair if it's the latter. He's the ringmaster of this three-ring televised circus.

But for Jonathan, who had spent much of his childhood being bullied because of his weight, it was perhaps even more of a signature moment.

"I've always had problems with my size since I could remember. When I was in … school, it damaged my confidence quite a bit. When people would say something to me, it would take a piece out of me in a sense."

Jonathan, who weighed about 280 pounds when he competed on *Britain's Got Talent*, said he had been dealing with weight issues as long as he could remember — he was first classified as overweight at age 4 or 5.

"Ever since I was quite small I've had problems and the bullying was related to that," he said. "People would be nasty about my weight and say nasty words."

It wasn't a case of physical violence.

"No one ever hit me; I wouldn't have allowed them to," he said. "That's the one thing — I'm a big guy and I could hit back. But someone who once asked me how much I weighed decided to test it by sitting on me so I couldn't get up."

He left the public school he had attended for several years, transferring to a private school. But the move backfired. He found himself faced with a heavier load of homework, in addition to choir practice before school and more rehearsals afterward. He had little time for anything beyond school, homework, rehearsals and sleep.

He suffered bouts of insomnia and depression that eventually led to a nervous breakdown.

"My life just felt pointless," he said. "I had suicidal thoughts. It was a serious thing. I was a danger to myself. I would self-harm. I'd cut my arms and torso. I thought about it (suicide) constantly for two months."

He eventually left school altogether.

"Me and school just don't get on," the teen said. "That's just the way it's always been. I've never felt right there."

At least one good thing did come out of Jonathan's educational experience, though. It was there that he met Charlotte, during a singing class at Essex secondary school. It was also there that they were paired by a music teacher who realized their voices would complement each other.

The teacher, Ginette Brown, had an ulterior motive for suggesting that they learn *The Prayer* by Celine Dion and Andrea Bocelli: she hoped they would one day sing it at her wedding. They eventually did so, performing the piece at her wedding to business studies teacher David Brown.

They also performed it for their class final (they got an "A," naturally).

"I chose *The Prayer* because I thought it would showcase their talents," Brown said. "I thought it was a beautiful piece. I hoped they would sing it at my wedding, to about 100 people. I never imagined that one day I would be sitting in my lounge watching two very dear students, whom I had seen grow up, singing that song to millions on national television."

Jonathan, however, was shy. Charlotte, by contrast, was confident and outgoing. Her support had helped Jonathan through the years, and it was her idea that the pair apply to perform on *Britain's Got Talent* — where they would reprise their performance of the Bocelli-Dion duet they had sung in school.

"I'm quite protective of Jonathan," Charlotte said. "If I was there and someone said something (rude) to him, I couldn't sit there with my mouth shut. … Before you make a judgment of someone, you really need to get to know them."

Before his triumphant appearance on *Britain's Got Talent*, Jonathan's mother said he would rarely leave the house. Indeed, she said, he would never have been able to go through with his appearance on the show if it hadn't been for Charlotte's support: "He'd never had managed to sing for Simon Cowell if he hadn't had Charlotte by his side."

No wonder he wasn't about to abandon her.

Of course, it didn't hurt that she was impressive as a singer in her own right.

The title of their debut CD puts an emphatic exclamation mark on that point.

It's titled *Together*.

"All the students of all years would see him and say: 'That's Jonathan Antoine, the boy with the incredible voice.'"

— Ginette Brown

Lady Gaga
Born This Way

Jonathan Antoine isn't alone. As a matter of fact, some people might be surprised to find out how many famous people have been bullied.

Steve Jobs, the founder of Apple Inc., was obviously a smart guy. So it's no surprise that he skipped a grade in school. As a result, however, he was smaller than his classmates, who made a habit of picking on him.

His status as a loner didn't help, and the situation eventually became so bad that the 11-year-old Jobs came home and told his parents he was never going to that school again. They listened. Jobs' family soon moved from their working-class neighborhood to Palo Alto, where he attended Cupertino Junior High and joined the Hewlett-Packard Explorer Club.

His interest in computers was kindled, setting the stage for his future success.

Actress Sandra Bullock recalled being bullied at school because of the way her mother — German opera singer Helga Meyer — dressed her: "I'd come back from Europe and I looked like a clown compared to the way the other students looked and dressed," she said. "So I got my ass whooped a little bit. Kids are mean, and the sad thing is that I can still remember the first and last names of every one of those kids who were mean to me."

Olympic swimming champ Michael Phelps was teased because he had a lisp and his ears stuck out.

As the only black student in his New York school, comedian Chris Rock recalls getting called the N word and beaten up "every day."

Kate Winslet of *Titanic* fame was teased because of her weight. So was singer Demi Lovato. Singer Rihanna was bulled because of her light skin. Actress Eva Mendes was teased because she was "a gawky, skinny girl with big teeth."

Add the performer once known as Stefani Germanotta to the list, as well.

Never heard of her? A few years back, Germanotta ditched that name and adopted another moniker: Lady Gaga. Under that name, the singer-songwriter rocketed to stardom in 2008 with a debut album appropriately titled *The Fame*. Now, she wants to make sure the problem of bullying and its devastating effects are just as well-known as she is.

In 2011, Gaga and her mother, Cynthia, founded the Born This Way Foundation, which seeks "to foster a more accepting society, where differences are embraced and individuality is celebrated."

Gaga's individuality wasn't always celebrated. Often, it was held against her.

"I was called really horrible, profane names very loudly in front of huge crowds of people, and my schoolwork suffered at one point," she told Nicholas Kristof in *The New York Times*. "I did not want to go to class. And I was a straight-A student, so there was a certain point in my high school years where I just couldn't even focus on class because I was so embarrassed all the time. I was so ashamed of who I was."

The bullying wasn't just verbal. At one point, she was thrown into a trash can.

The message was unmistakable.

You're different.

Conform, or else.

Become part of the crowd and don't stand out. You say you were born this way? Well, that's no excuse. If you can't conform, you'll have to be marginalized, discredited, ostracized and ridiculed. We can't have your influence infecting society as a whole with your differentness.

Raised in an Italian-American household, the girl who would become Lady Gaga "wanted to be a skinny little ballerina" but was instead a "voluptuous little Italian girl whose dad had meatballs on the table every night."

Gaga had always been musical and theatrical. She had begun studying the piano at age 4 and had earned the lead role in some high school theater productions and even got a bit part on an episode of the HBO series *The Sopranos*. At her mother's suggestion, she applied a musical theatre conservatory in New York and was accepted at 17.

But two years later, frustrated with the direction her life was taking, she decided to change it. It was then that she left school to pursue a career in music.

"I was very depressed when I was 19," she recalled. "I would go back to my apartment every day and I would just sit there. It was quiet and it was lonely. It was still. It was just my piano and myself. I had a television and would leave it on all the time just to feel like somebody was hanging out with me."

Gaga had the ultimate comeback. Like most innovators, she found success not by fitting in but by standing out. After forming the Stefani Germanotta Band and playing in Greenwich Village bars and lounges for a time, she made another crucial decision: she changed her image to become a daring trendsetter in both music and fashion, transforming her musical act into a vibrant, multidimensional assault on the senses.

"I live halfway between reality and theater at all times," she once said.

Other musicians had seen success following a theatrical formula: David Bowie, Elton John, KISS, Madonna, Queen. It's even been reported that Germanotta was inspired by the latter band to rebrand herself as Lady Gaga, taking her cue from Queen's hit *Radio Ga Ga*. (Queen singer Freddie Mercury himself had been a target during his school years: "I learned to fend for myself in boarding school. All the bullying and everything else.")

Four years later, Gaga had won five Grammy awards and ranked as the fourth-bestselling digital artist of all time. She was in the perfect position to spearhead an effort that would expose the cruelty of bullying, spotlight its devastating effects and provide a path to overcoming it by celebrating individuality.

Gaga became one of the nation's most vocal and visible advocates of free expression, individual dignity and equality. She has fought for — and continues to fight for — these principles across a broad spectrum of issues, including advocacy for the fair treatment of immigrants and LGBT rights. She complemented her efforts to empower youth against bullying with a campaign to fight stereotypes based on body type.

Bullies, she knows, target people for a variety of reasons.

"You don't have to be the loser kid in high school to be bullied," she said. "Bullying and being picked on comes in many forms."

As for Gaga?

"When I wake up in the morning, I feel just like any other insecure 24-year-old girl."

"I feel like if you're a really good human being, you can try to find something beautiful in every single person, no matter what."

— Lady Gaga

Susan LaFlesche Picotte
'We Are Not Driftwood'

Susan LaFlesche watched helplessly as the woman sick woman's condition grew worse. She tried to comfort her but had no way to heal her, so she sent a messenger to the local doctor.

The messenger returned, saying he would be along shortly.

But when he failed to appear and the woman continued to grow weaker, Susan sent him again. She was just a girl, but she knew that the ailing woman would not get better without help. Again the messenger returned with an assurance that the doctor would be there soon.

So she waited.

Twice more she sent the messenger, and twice more he returned with the same response. But the doctor never came ... and the woman died.

"It was only an Indian, and it did not matter," Susan LaFlesche Picotte later recalled. "The doctor preferred hunting for prairie chickens rather than visiting the poor, suffering humanity."

In the mid-19th century, medical care among the Omaha of Nebraska — a people who gave their name to that state's largest city — could best be described as basic. Contact with white Americans had been minimal until the Gold Rush of 1848 sent them westward to California in droves, and the region was made a territory six years later, 11 years before LaFlesche was born.

The newcomers had medical knowledge the Omaha lacked, but they seemed to care little for sharing it with people they arrogantly viewed as inferior.

LaFlesche's accomplishments would prove that arrogance badly misplaced.

Her father, Chief Joseph "Iron Eyes" LaFlesche — who lost his own leg to an untreated infection — understood that the Omaha would not be able to defeat the white settlers and told his daughter it would be best to learn from them. He had been among the leaders who signed treaties in Washington, D.C., creating the reservation in 1854. He had seen the large homes the settlers had built, and resolved to build one himself — a two-story wood-frame home that he presented as a model for others among the Omaha to emulate.

The old ways were changing. There was much to be gained from embracing the new.

"It matters not where one looks, now one sees white people," Iron Eye said. When she was just 6 years old, he asked her and her sisters a question that would shape her life: "Do you want to simply be called 'those Indians,' or do you want to go to school and be somebody in the world?"

The answer was clear in LaFlesche's mind.

She later wrote: "From that moment, I determined to make something useful of myself."

Susan ultimately left home to get an education, attending the Elizabeth Institute for Young Ladies in New Jersey and the Hampton Normal and Agricultural Institute in Virginia. Then she set her sights on medical school. There was no doubt she had both the motivation and intellect necessary to succeed. According to Hampton's principal Samuel Armstrong, she was "the finest, strongest Indian character we have ever had at the school."

Still, there were social hurdles to overcome — few women of any race aspired to be physicians, a job traditionally reserved for men — and then there was the matter of tuition to consider.

Enlisting the help of the Connecticut Indian Association, a women's group and the government, LaFlesche secured the $167 yearly tuition fee plus clothing, along with room and board. She was the first person ever to receive U.S. government funding to pursue higher education.

It proved a wise investment when she graduated tops in her class of 36 from Women's Medical College in Pennsylvania. Eventually, she returned to the reservation and, after being turned down at her first request, was accepted to the position of reservation doctor. Initially, some distrusted her as someone who had left the reservation and been educated in white schools.

Was she a traitor to her heritage? Would she be unable to understand their medical needs?

The answer to both questions was a resounding "no." LaFlesche quickly earned the trust of those on the reservation when she successfully treated an 8-year-old boy for a childhood ailment. A day after his doctor's appointment, the youngster was up and about, playing like any other perfectly healthy Omaha boy in a nearby creek.

Soon, she was seeing not only Omaha clients, but white patients as well.

It wasn't an easy life by any means. She worked out of a building with less than 200 square feet of space that doubled as a community hall. Her salary was just $500. Accounting for inflation, that would be the equivalent of roughly $12,000 in the early 21st century. One can scarcely imagine a modern American doctor functioning on a salary that's right at today's poverty level.

Making matters worse, she had to dip into her own pocket to pay for medical supplies when the government ran out.

To earn this meager salary, LaFlesche kept up a rigorous schedule that taxed her strength but not her determination. And yes, she made house calls — riding on horseback across the length and breadth of a reservation that spanned more than 450 square miles, sometimes in subfreezing temperatures. "My office hours are any and all hours of the day or night," she said.

Her efforts were heroic, and they continued even as she battled the degenerative bone disease that would eventually take her life. Her reasoning was simple: "The Omaha's depend on me."

So they did.

The U.S. government had decided that the Omahas were incapable of looking after their own affairs and held their property in trust. Members of the Omaha nation who wanted to rent their land hand to receive permission from Uncle Sam to do so, regardless of their financial needs. This entailed traveling long distances to file an appeal and appear before a panel, then waiting for the matter to be decided.

Sometimes, people's lives were forfeit to the bureaucracy. LaFlesche saw one woman die of tuberculosis while waiting for the government to release the funds to which she was entitled.

The year was 1910. LaFlesche had married Henry Picotte and set up a private practice in Bancroft, Neb., some years earlier, but she continued to advocate for the Omaha. When he died in 1905, she became a Presbyterian missionary to the Omaha nation and their representative to the U.S. government. Five years later — although her illness had progressed to the point that she could barely stand — she accepted a plea from her people to advocate for them in Washington. The government, it seemed, had announced it planned to extend the burdensome trust.

Speaking before the secretary of the interior and the U.S. attorney general, Picotte did not mince words: "We are not stones. We are not driftwood. We have feelings, hopes, ambitions and aspirations," she declared. "We have suffered enough from your experiments — we have been practically robbed of our rights by the government. In the name of justice and humanity, we ask for a more liberal interpretation of the law."

As a result of her efforts, the government agreed to end the trust.

Her dream, however, was to see a hospital built on the reservation, a modern medical center that would be a far cry from the tiny makeshift office from which she had once worked. In 1913, that dream became a reality thanks to money she raised from various sources. The entire east side of the main floor was a colonnaded open porch equipped with hammocks — a place where patients could recover in the fresh air and sunshine.

It was the first hospital on any reservation not built using government money.

"When the new hospital is built, in the spring, then we will rejoice," Picotte wrote shortly before its opening, "for it will give the Indians a chance to receive proper care during sickness."

And so it did.

Even in her declining health, Picotte served as head of the 17-bed hospital in its first years. Renamed in her honor shortly after her death in 1915, it remained in use as a working hospital for more than a quarter-century before being used as an elder-care center. It was named a National Historic Landmark in 1993 and converted into a museum with exhibits highlighting her work and the history of the Omaha and Winnebago nations.

"You can never push an Omaha down or pass a thing over his head; he will light on his feet facing you."

— Susan LaFlesche Picotte

Kenny Washington
West Coast Legend

Jackie Robinson was never a star baseball player in college. In fact, he probably should have given up on the sport — and not because of the color barrier. The plain truth of the matter is that Robinson wasn't particularly good ... and he was dynamite in three other sports: track and field, basketball and football.

In track, he followed in the footsteps of his older brother Mack, who had won a silver medal in the 200 meters at the 1936 Olympics. The man who beat Mack Robinson was none other than Jesse Owens, who finished just four-tenths of a second faster. So it should have come as little surprise when younger brother Jackie won the national championship in the long jump four years later.

What may surprise modern readers is that the younger Robinson didn't seem to be cut out for baseball. In his only season at UCLA, he batted an anemic .097.

On the basketball court, however, it was a different story. He was the top scorer in the Pacific Coast Conference's Southern Division two years running. And on the football field, he was even better. During his senior season, he led the Bruins in no fewer than five categories: total offense, scoring, rushing, passing and punt returns. In the last of these, he averaged an astonishing 18.8 yards over his career — fourth best in NCAA history.

Robinson seemed destined to play pro football, and indeed he joined the semipro Honolulu Bears and later the Los Angeles

Bulldogs of the Pacific Coast Football League. But World War II intervened — Robinson was actually sailing home after an exhibition game in Pearl Harbor when the Japanese attacked. He played some games with the Bulldogs but was drafted into the Army and served for the next two years before receiving an honorable discharge in 1944.

Upon rejoining civilian life, Robinson returned to the football field for the L.A. Bulldogs and picked up right where he left off. In his first game, against the San Francisco Packers, the threw a pair of touchdown passes. In his next, against crosstown rival Hollywood, he ran for three scores and 108 yards on just eight carries.

That set up a showdown with the undefeated San Diego Bombers on Nov. 26, 1944, but Robinson touched the ball just once before injuring his ankle. He never played another down of football. Instead, the following year, he accepted a contract offer to play baseball for the Kansas City Monarchs of the Negro Leagues. He hit a team-leading .414 while playing shortstop for the Monarchs that year, and by 1947 he had become the first African-American player in the major leagues during the 20th century.

Everyone knows that story.

What many people don't know is that Robinson wasn't the only black player on the UCLA football team, and that — despite his impressive credentials — he may not even have been the best. His teammate Kenny Washington rushed for 1,914 yards during his collegiate career, a figure that stood as a school record for 34 years.

Washington's father, ironically, had played for the Kansas City Monarchs himself. But it was his son who would become the family's most famous athlete. How good was he? All you had to do was ask Jackie Robinson, who himself described Washington as "the greatest football player I've ever seen. He had everything needed for greatness — size, speed and tremendous strength. Kenny was probably the greatest long passer ever."

That wasn't hyperbole. During a game against crosstown rival Southern Cal in 1937, Washington threw a pass that traveled 62 yards in the air for a touchdown. And he would only get better. As a senior two years later, he led the nation in total yards, with Montana coach Doug Fessenden pronouncing him "greater than Red Grange." With Washington playing both offense and defense — he was on the field all but 20 minutes the entire season — the Bruins went undefeated that year and were kept out of the Rose Bowl only by a scoreless tie with Southern Cal.

Amazingly, Washington was not selected to play in the East-West Shrine Game (an all-star game showcasing the nation's best collegiate players), nor was he chosen first-team All-America. Despite these snubs, however, he almost became the first player drafted into the National Football League straight out of college.

Almost.

Washington was chosen to play on a team of college all-stars in an annual exhibition game against the NFL champions — in this case, the Green Bay Packers. The Packers won the game 45-28, but Washington scored a touchdown and so impressed Chicago Bears owner George Halas that he asked Washington to stick around for a couple of weeks. His intent was to persuade his fellow owners that the time had come to break the color barrier ... so he could draft Washington.

He convinced all but one: George Preston Marshall of the Washington Redskins. But that was enough to keep Washington out of the NFL and send him back to Los Angeles, where he began playing for the Hollywood Bears — rival to Robinson's Los Angeles Bulldogs in the semipro Pacific Coast Football League.

Washington was so popular his team was sometimes billed as "Kenny Washington and the Hollywood Bears" (the name Bears having been chosen as a professional counterpart to the UCLA Bruins mascot). He was injured and missed two games in 1940, when the Bears placed second behind the Bulldogs, but was healthy in 1941 and led the Bears to the championship on the strength of an undefeated season.

Injuries again kept Washington off the field — and out of the war — for the next two years, before he returned to action with the San Francisco Clippers of the American Football League (a rival West Coast circuit that used the name 15 years before the advent of the better-known pro league). He helped the Clippers to a second-place finish before returning the following season to the Bears when the AFL collapsed.

In 1945, Washington appeared to be back in top form, taking the Bears to another title while he personally led the league in scoring. He also ranked second and third in rushing and passing respectively and once again grabbed the attention of the pro leagues. This time, it wasn't George Halas of the Bears but Dan Reeves of the defending champion Rams who came calling … but not without a little encouragement.

When Reeves, the owner of the team, announced he was moving to Los Angeles, other owners were less than pleased. They tried to block the move by denying his request. But it wasn't just a request. Reeves wouldn't take "no" for an answer and announced that he'd quit the league altogether if his fellow owners didn't reconsider their position. They might have let him do it, too, except for the fact that another pro football league was forming — and planned to include a franchise in Los Angeles.

Fearful of this nascent challenge, the NFL gave in to Reeves' ultimatum and approved the transfer.

Next, the Rams would have to find a place to play. The city's showcase stadium was the Memorial Coliseum, which had been built for the 1932 Olympic Games, so the team's owner and general manager set up a meeting with the county commission to secure a lease.

It wouldn't be that easy.

As it turned out, an African-American sportswriter named Halley Harding of the *Los Angeles Tribune* also showed up at the meeting. Black tax dollars had helped build the Coliseum, he said, so no team making use of it should be allowed to discriminate. He called George

Preston Marshall — the owner who had kept Washington out of football six years earlier — the handmaiden of Jim Crow pro football. And he said it was "singularly strange" that no NFL team had signed Washington.

Harding made a persuasive argument — one that was joined by the commission itself: What about Washington? Wasn't he the city's biggest football star for the past decade? Would the Rams give him a tryout?

Reeves and the Rams were backed into a corner. They were already committed to playing in Los Angeles, and the publicly owned Coliseum was the obvious venue of choice. But the commission's unspoken message was clear: Washington would get a tryout (and a spot on the team), or the Rams could get lost.

Unfortunately, the Kenny Washington who joined the Rams in 1946 wasn't the same athlete who had led UCLA to an undefeated season seven years earlier. Several knee injuries had taken their toll, and he had undergone surgery at least twice. When he signed with the Rams, he was preparing for another operation on the knee, and he saw limited action in his first season.

Not only did he have to battle his bad knees, but he also had to face racism on the field.

"When he first began to play, they'd tee off on him," Rams backfield coach Bob Snyder told the *Chicago Sun-Times*. "They'd drop knees on him."

In a game against the Washington Redskins, several players reportedly piled on top of him and rubbed chalk in his eyes. In another game, a tackle for the Green Bay Packers slammed an elbow into Washington's jaw. Washington recovered and started talking to the guy.

When Rams Snyder asked halfback Tom Harmon — the former Heisman Trophy winner and future TV announcer — what had happened, he told the coach: "That guy called Kenny a black bastard. Kenny started at him and then he got his composure, and he said, 'Listen, that was a pretty good shot.' And then he said, 'I want to tell you something, you white trash. If you want to wait till the game is over, meet me under the stadium and I'll knock your goddamn block off.'"

Washington only played three seasons in the NFL before retiring in 1948, but he left his mark. During his second season, he led the league with an average of 7.4 yards per carry for a total of 444 yards, including a 92-yard scoring run in a win over the eventual league champions, the Chicago Cardinals. The Rams were one of only three teams to beat the Cardinals that year.

On retiring, he tried baseball for a time, attending a tryout with the New York Giants and playing a few games at first base for the Los Angeles Angels of the Pacific Coast League before retiring from sports for good and settling into a career with the Los Angeles Police Department.

When he died in 1971 of arterial disease, his number had been retired at UCLA and he had been inducted into the College Football Hall of Fame. But his relatively short NFL career — and the racism that preceded it — kept him from the greater recognition he so richly deserved as the man who broke the color barrier in America's most popular sport.

Rams quarterback Bob Waterfield made it plain what so many American football fans missed out on: "If he had come into the NFL directly from UCLA, he would have been, in my opinion, the best the NFL had ever seen."

"As I look back on it now, it was just as important for a colored player to break into pro football as it was in baseball."

— Kenny Washington

Mildred and Richard Loving
The Loving Thing to Do

Why can't they just leave it alone?
Why make waves?
Do you really have to make a scene?

These are some of the questions that get asked whenever someone decides to challenge a system they find unfair, corrupt or antiquated. The thing is, they simply don't apply. People who have been targeted for bias or bullying aren't trying to make waves; just the opposite — they're trying to navigate away from what sometimes seems like a tsunami of bitterness and cruelty.

Most have no illusions about changing the world; they just want to change *their* world.

Take the case of Mildred Jeter and Richard Loving. All they wanted to do was get married. In 1950, approximately 1.7 million people in the United States had tied the knot. Now, it was eight years later, and this couple from Virginia wanted to do the same. It was a simple concept. Their request didn't involve bigamy or incest, and both of them were adults — Loving was 24, and Jeter was just about to turn 19.

So they went to Washington, D.C., in June of 1958, filled out a marriage license and were married.

Then the newlyweds returned home to Virginia ... where they were arrested a little more than a month later. The county sheriff and a pair of deputies — acting on an anonymous tip — raided their home at 2 in the morning, barging into the Lovings' bedroom and treating them like suspected drug dealers or terrorists.

"Who is this woman you're sleeping with?" the sheriff demanded.

"I'm his wife," Mildred replied.

She pointed to their marriage certificate, which was displayed on the wall, but the sheriff was unmoved.

"That's no good here," he said brusquely. He and the deputies then took the Lovings into custody and summarily threw them in jail for violating something called the "Racial Integrity Act," a law passed in 1924 that barred interracial marriage. Richard spent one night there; Mildred — who was pregnant at the time — was forced to stay longer.

Even though they had been legally married, the Virginia law barred them from "cohabiting as man and wife, against the peace and dignity of the Commonwealth." The phrase was perversely ironic, because the Lovings wanted nothing more than peace and dignity for themselves. They weren't out to raise a ruckus or set a precedent. They wanted nothing more than to live together as husband and wife.

It must have been like buying a car, then being told that you have to leave it parked in a garage. Someone else's garage. Across the state line. But even that's a bad analogy: a spouse is infinitely more precious than a car.

None of that mattered, though. What mattered was the color of their skin, and when the Lovings appeared in court, the judge threw the book at them. The Bible, that is — or, rather, his skewed interpretation of it. "Almighty God created the races white, black, yellow, malay, and red," he wrote in his verdict for the Circuit Court of Caroline County. "The fact that he separated the races shows that he did not intend for the races to mix."

The judge apparently ignored the biblical idea that all human life could be traced to a single couple, not to mention the injunction of Jesus in the book of Matthew: "What God has joined together, let no one separate." On the contrary, Judge Leon Bazile was hell-bent on separating the married couple who stood before him. (And the constitutional separation of church and state be damned.)

Bazile sentenced them to a year in prison but offered to suspend their sentences if they would leave the state — in effect sending them into exile for 25 years. Finding themselves with little choice in the matter, the couple moved to the District of Columbia, away from friends and family, and settled down to live the sort of life typical of a married couple. Richard found work as a bricklayer. They had kids (three of them).

After a few years, however, they grew tired of living away from the state they had been their home — and returning separately on rare occasions just to see their loved ones. So they contacted Attorney General Robert Kennedy, who referred her to the American Civil Liberties Union. There, they worked with Bernard Cohen, an attorney who was volunteering for the group.

"They were very simply people who were not interested in winning any civil rights principle," Cohen later recalled. "They were just in love with one another and wanted the right to live together as husband and wife in Virginia. ... When I told Richard that this case was, in all likelihood, going to the Supreme Court of the United States, he became wide-eyed and his jaw dropped."

Still, it took a while to get there.

When petitioned to set aside his previous ruling, Bazile refused. Next it was the turn of the Virginia Supreme Court of Appeals, where Justice Harry L. Carrico sided with Bazile and refused the Lovings' request. From there, it went to the U.S. Supreme Court, which finally heard the case on April 10, 1967, more than eight years after the couple exchanged vows.

The Lovings didn't attend the hearing, but Richard Loving sent along a message: "Tell the court I love my wife, and it's just unfair that I can't live with her in Virginia."

Three months after those arguments, the Supreme Court unanimously ruled in favor of the Lovings, striking down Virginia's racist law and also voiding similar laws in 15 other states.

"I feel free," Richard Loving is said to have declared.

The couple moved back to Virginia, where they built a home and began raising their children, Donald, Peggy and Sidney. They lived together there for the next eight years until 1975, when a traffic accident involving a drunken driver claimed Richard's life. Mildred, who was in the car with him at the time, lost vision in her right eye.

Richard Loving was just 41 when he died; Mildred lived to the age of 68, dying of pneumonia in 2008.

A year earlier, on the 40th anniversary of the Supreme Court decision, she issued a statement on the historic case that shattered the legal barrier to interracial marriage. It concluded as follows:

"Surrounded as I am by wonderful children and grandchildren, not a day goes by that I don't think of Richard and our love, our right to marry, and how much it meant to me to have the freedom to marry the person precious to me, even if others thought he was the 'wrong kind of person' for me to marry. I believe all Americans, no matter their race, no matter their sex, no matter their sexual orientation, should have the freedom to marry. Government has no business imposing religious beliefs over others. Especially if it denies people's civil rights... I support the freedom to marry for all. That's what Loving, and loving, are all about."

"We loved each other and got married. We are not marrying the state. The law should allow a person to marry who he wants."

— Mildred Loving

Shahin Najafi

A Price on His Head

He's not apologizing.

In May 2012, Iranian rapper Shahin Najafi released a song titled *Naqi*, invoking the name of Shia Islam's tenth imam in a critique of Iranian society. In response, an anonymous cleric placed a $100,000 price on his head — a fatwa that was promoted online — and Najafi went into hiding.

Rap isn't a genre of music known for pulling punches. It's known for rough, often confrontational language, and the autocratic regime in Iran doubtless found it unacceptable to be on the receiving end of such a critique. The song itself doesn't actually insult the tenth imam at all; on the contrary, it calls for him to return and address the corruption in the Iranian regime.

The song derides the government's "shallow slogans" and "Chinese-made prayer rugs."

There's no sexism.

No violence.

Just political commentary. And that's where the problem lies, at least from the Iranian government's perspective. One lyric, for example, derides the late Ayatollah Khomeini (who issued a similar death-sentence fatwa against author Salman Rushdie more than two decades earlier) as the "cardboard ayatollah."

Though Najafi is known in some quarters as the "Iranian Eminem" and both artists offer satirical, frequently biting social commentary, his lyrics tend more toward social issues. Whereas Eminem may skewer various pop culture icons and lay bare his own personal struggles, Najafi addresses topics such as poverty, child labor, sexism, executions and theocracy.

The use of the imam's name, Najafi said, was just an excuse for the Iranian regime to marginalize and attempt to silence him. Those in power, he said, "are taking advantage of the situation to make it look like I was trying to criticize religion and put down believers."

Hence, the fatwa.

Fatwas are judicial rulings by Muslim clerics or authoritative religious scholars. They can apply to a broad variety of issues, most of them rather ordinary and narrowly applied. This one is potentially lethal.

"The lyrics are provocative," Najafi admitted in a German radio interview, "but there is no verse, not a single word that insults religion. I tell him (the tenth imam) he should not hesitate to do away with the many misfeatures in the country: with oppression and sexual violence, with the trend of cosmetic surgery, and with imported cheap goods that are flooding the Iranian market."

Apparently, such criticisms hit a little too close to home for the Iranian regime, which began promoting a campaign online to have Najafi hanged. It's not the first time he's been on their bad side. In fact, Najafi left Iran for Germany in 2005 rather than bow to pressure from a government demanding that he purge his music of political content.

Instead, he joined a band called Tapesh 2012 — another group blacklisted by the establishment in Iran. The conservative newspaper Kayhan, for example, asserted that the members of Tapesh use "vulgar songs and create sexual attraction to attract students to oppose the regime."

Najafi left Tapesh in 2009 but continued to produce songs laced with blunt political commentary targeting conditions in Iran. He's banned from performing in his home country, and his recordings are only available on the black market, though they can also be downloaded online.

Now, he has been placed under a death sentence.

"Their aim is to create fear, intimidation and terror among people and for me, so that I don't continue with my work and people become fearful that they could be persecuted for listening to my music," Najafi told *The Daily Beast*. Although he expressed fears for his own safety as a result of the fatwa, he was steadfast that he had no regrets about stating his views.

"Each person has a price to pay for what they want," he said. "I will never apologize for my art and for speaking the truth about Iran's government."

*"Fundamentalists can't take a joke. Ever.
They want us to blindly obey, parrot everything they do,
believe in their dogmas."*

— Shahin Najafi

Viktor Frankl
Transforming Tragedy

"For the first time in my life, I saw the truth as it is set into song by so many poets, proclaimed as the final wisdom by so many thinkers. The truth — that love is the ultimate and highest goal to which man can aspire."

These were the words of Viktor Frankl, a man who became a noted neurologist, psychiatrist and author — and, for nearly three years, a prisoner in German concentration camps.

Frankl was a man of great accomplishment long before World War II began. While still a teenager, he entered into a series of correspondences with Sigmund Freud, and upon completing his secondary education enrolled at the University of Vienna. There he studied neurology and psychology, with an emphasis on depression and suicide.

After Hitler invaded his native Austria in 1938, he had a chance to flee to the United States. He obtained a visa but allowed it to expire because he feared for his elderly parents. It was a fateful decision, as both his parents would die in German concentration camps — his father of starvation at Theresienstadt in Bohemia, and his mother in the gas chambers at Auschwitz.

Frankl doubtless had reason to hope. Although he was of Jewish ancestry, he had been appointed as chief of the neurological department at Rothschilds Hospital in 1940.

50 UNDEFEATED

It was the only hospital for Jews in Vienna during the Nazi occupation. While there, he purposely wrote false diagnoses for several patients in order to subvert Nazi laws requiring euthanasia for the mentally ill.

Less than two years later, he married Tilly Grosser, but they lived together less than a year before Frankl was relieved of his post at the hospital and deported to the Theresienstadt camp in what is now the Czech Republic. Frankl's father died there. So did tens of thousands of other Jews.

Frankl continued his work at Theresienstadt, but two years later he was moved again. This time, he and his wife were separated — he was sent to a camp called Kaufering, and she to Bergen-Belsen. He spent the next five months as a slave laborer before he was transferred again and eventually liberated by American forces in April of 1945. But he never saw his wife again.

She died at Bergen-Belsen.

His brother Walter, meanwhile, perished while working at a mine associated with Auschwitz. Of Frankl's family, only he and a sister who had emigrated to Australia before the war remained alive.

Frankl would later reflect on his experiences in *Man's Search for Meaning*, a book he dictated in just nine days.

In it, he would declare: "We who lived in concentration camps can remember the men who walked through the huts comforting others, giving away their last piece of bread. They may have been few in number, but they offer sufficient proof that everything can be taken from a man but one thing: the last of the human freedoms — to choose one's attitude in any given set of circumstances, to choose one's own way."

Frankl continued to make his own way for the next half-century. He returned to Vienna, where he took a teaching position at the University of Vienna Medical School — a post he held for 25 years. Three years after the war ended, he received a Ph.D. in philosophy and, two years later, he founded the Austrian Medical Society for Psychotherapy.

He climbed mountains, remarried and took up flying, earning his pilot's license at the age of 67. He continued teaching, meanwhile, until the age of 85.

What matters, he said, "is to bear witness to the uniquely human potential at its best, which is to transform a personal tragedy into a triumph, to turn one's predicament into a human achievement."

Frankl didn't just say this.

He lived it.

"When we are no longer able to change a situation, we are challenged to change ourselves."

— Viktor Frankl

STEPHEN H. PROVOST

Krystal Myers
Daring to Disbelieve

Krystal Myers just wanted to express her faith — or, rather, her lack of it. The senior at Lenoir City High School in Tennessee saw Christian students saying prayers at football games and wearing religious T-shirts; there were even quotes from the Bible displayed on classroom bulletin boards.

Now, she wanted to offer her own perspective.

Myers was no slouch. She was an honors student involved in school government and captain of the swim team. As editor of the student newspaper, she thought her ideas would be protected under the First Amendment when she penned an editorial calling for equal treatment. Instead, the school proved her point for her.

It refused to publish the piece.

The school director, Wayne Miller, said Myers' column was kept out of the *Panther Press* because of the potential for disruption at Lenoir City High. Miller told the *Knoxville News Sentinel*: "We do have the right to control the content of the school paper if it is in the best interest of the students."

Clearly, it wasn't in Myers' best interest. And if school officials wanted to censor her opinions, their efforts backfired in the extreme when Myers took her column to the *News Sentinel* — which promptly published it. A bit of perspective: Lenoir City High's student population was listed at 1,300, while the News Sentinel's circulation was more than 75 times as large at nearly 100,000.

One purpose of Myers' column was "to clear up some misconceptions about atheism."

"No," she wrote, "we don't worship the 'devil.' We do not believe in God, so we also do not believe in Satan. And we may be 'godless,' but that does not mean that we are without morals. I know I strive to be the best person I can be, even without religion." Denying the existence of God, she added, "does not mean that atheists do not believe in higher causes; we just do not believe in a higher being."

It's hard to see how school officials could find it disruptive to clear up misconceptions and advocate for high moral standards — or, for that matter, to advocate for constitutional freedom, something else Myers did in her letter. In appealing to the First Amendment, she argued against the establishment of religion at her school.

"The Christian faith cannot rule the United States," she stated. "It is unconstitutional. Religion and government are supposed to be separate. If we let this slide, what other amendments to the Constitution will be ignored."

It was an appropriate question. In asserting her own rights to be free of established religion under the First Amendment, Myers found herself being stripped of other First Amendment protections: freedom of speech and freedom of the press. While schools do have a right to exercise oversight of student publications, they don't have a right show favoritism in deciding to exclude material.

Some in the community, however, didn't see it that way. A comment thread sprang up online titled "Krystal Myers should be Excommunicated from the City and County." One commenter called her lewd names; another suggested that she be taken outside the city and stoned.

"They are not too happy with me, and now everyone seems to know who I am," Myers said. "I was expecting some negative feedback, but nothing to this extent."

Myers wasn't the only target of the community backlash against her commentary. School newspaper advisor Richard Yoakley, who had supported her right to submit the piece for publication, was summoned to the principal's office. He later got in more trouble as advisor to the school yearbook, which included an article about a gay student at Lenoir High. "The administration," he said, "didn't talk to me for two weeks" and subsequently asked him to resign on the grounds that he was "improperly influencing" students.

Shortly after he refused, he was transferred to another school.

None of this was, by any means, unprecedented.

Myers wasn't the first student writer to face this sort of backlash for daring to disbelieve — and to defend that disbelief in public. Two centuries earlier, the same kind of prejudice was directed against English poet and atheist Percy Bysshe Shelley.

Shelley was 18, the same age as Myers, when he enrolled at the prestigious University of Oxford. He came from Eton College, where he had been bullied mercilessly by classmates who repeatedly tore his clothes and knocked the books from his hands.

Yet books would be Shelley's weapon to answer them.

Within a year, he had published two novels and a pamphlet called *The Necessity of Atheism*. It was this latter work, a relatively short piece about the same length as Krystal Myers' column, that would get him in hot water with the authorities at Oxford less than a year after he enrolled.

Having made the acquaintance of a fellow student named Thomas Jefferson Hogg in the dining hall one day, he struck up a conversation that led first to a friendship and ultimately to the pamphlet in question.

In it, Shelley listed three ways in which one might argue for the existence of a deity: evidence from the senses, from reason and from testimony. Having dismissed each of these three arguments as inadequate, he concluded that, "having no proofs from any of the three sources of conviction: the mind *cannot* believe the existence of a God."

The pamphlet itself was produced anonymously, but Shelley himself promoted it vigorously at the university, as well as in London.

Not only was it distributed to the students and the public at large, but Shelley made a point of sending copies to all the important personages at Oxford: professors, bishops and even those in the highest positions of authority.

It should have come as no surprise that both Shelley and Hogg were called to account for their work. Each man was asked whether he was the author, and each man declined to say one way or the other. Their refusal to answer was taken as a sign of their responsibility in the matter, and both men were immediately expelled from the university.

Three days after being bounced out of Oxford, Shelley wrote his father, explaining that he and Hogg had found the supposed proofs of God's existence to be "defective" and had therefore written a simple essay concerning their conclusions.

"How then were we treated?" he asked. "Not as our fair, open, candid conduct might demand, no argument was brought forth to disprove our reasoning, and it at once demonstrated the weakness of their cause, and their inveteracy on discovering it, when they publicly expelled myself and my friend."

Shelley, however, received the same amount of sympathy from his father as he had from the powers at Oxford.

None.

Instead, the elder Shelley scrawled the word "impious" across his son's essay and confronted the teenager with "scolding, crying, swearing, and then weeping again." Further, he attempted to negotiate his son's return to Oxford — on the condition that he repudiate the essay that had got him in such hot water to begin with.

Shelley adamantly refused, and remained steadfast in that refusal with the passage of time. A year after his expulsion, he wrote, "My father's notions of family honour are incoincident with my knowledge of the public good. I will never sacrifice the latter to any consideration. My father has ever regarded me as a blot, a defilement of his honour."

History regarded Shelley somewhat more favorably. He went on to pen such works as the sonnet *Ozymandias* and the four-act drama *Prometheus Unbound*. Unfortunately, Shelley's works were largely ignored during his own brief lifetime — he drowned in a boating accident a month before his 30th birthday. After his death, however, he came to be admired by such notables as Henry David Thoreau, Upton Sinclair, Bertrand Russell, Oscar Wilde, George Bernard Shaw and W.B. Yeats.

A vegetarian and an advocate of nonviolent resistance to oppression, Shelley set forth ideas in his *Masque of Anarchy* that were often quoted by no less a figure than Mohandas K. Gandhi of India. (His second wife Mary even surpassed his fame, thanks to her novel *Frankenstein; or, The Modern Prometheus*, originally intended as a short story but expanded into a novel at Percy Shelley's suggestion. It was her first novel, and she published it at the age of 21.)

It is, in a way, amazing to note that so little has changed since Percy Shelley's short treatise on atheism caused such a stir at Oxford.

Three centuries later, a similar treatise by another gifted student in Tennessee caused a similar reaction by authorities who tried to censor it for the same basic reasons. If anything, Krystal Myers' commentary was less confrontational than Shelley's; whereas the Englishman set out to highlight the flaws of theism, the American writer wasn't interested in converting others to her position. On the contrary, she wanted *them* to stop trying to convert *her*.

Myers wrote that "perhaps the most important misconception is that we want to convert everyone to atheism and that we hate Christians. For the most part, we just want to be respected for who we are and not be judged."

Is that too much to ask?

"I leave you to decide what you will or will not do, but just remember that nonbelievers are not what you originally thought we were. We are human beings — just like you."

— Krystal Myers

Gleb Yakunin
Defender of the Faith

Persecution can cut both ways. Gleb Yakunin is living proof.

At one point in his life, the Russian-born priest found himself targeted by Soviet authorities for daring to practice Christianity in an atheist state. At another, he was targeted by the Russian Orthodox Church for daring to defy its directives. In both cases, he was banished — in the first case to a gulag; in the second instance from the church.

Yakunin was born in 1934 into a Soviet state that had done its best to exterminate religion. During the previous decade, clergy with the Russian Orthodox Church had been sent en masse to labor camps or simply shot. Some of the laity had suffered the same fate. Meanwhile, seminaries were closed, and only about 500 out of 50,000 churches remained open.

"Russia turned crimson with the blood of martyrs," Yakunin later said.

Christianity was simply not an option.

With the Nazi invasion of Russia, however, Soviet leader Joseph Stalin relaxed the nation's strict atheist stance and turned to the Orthodox Church as a rallying point in the war effort. Churches were reopened, and an official council was convened to elect a new patriarch of Moscow.

Still, the church was in many ways the handmaiden of the state. It existed at the pleasure of the Soviet regime, and its activities were tightly controlled to ensure that it reinforced the views of the ruling Communist Party.

Some Orthodox Christians, however, were unwilling to accept this subordinate status. Among them was Alexander Men, a member of the Catacomb Church. This organization had separated from the larger Orthodox Church three decades earlier over a demand that all church members to profess loyalty to the Soviet government. Those who refused had left the church and formed their own underground group.

Men's decision to affiliate with this church cost him dearly. He was expelled from college in 1958, and around this time made the acquaintance of Yakunin, who had studied biology at Irkutsk Agricultural Institute and soon found himself attracted to the same sort of faith that Men had embraced from childhood. "I find more meaning in the wing of a bird and in the branch of a tree than in five hundred icons," Men once said.

An intellectual leader, he lamented that "people do not want freedom. "People crave a freedomless Christianity; they particularly incline toward slavery."

Men, however, was inclined in the opposite direction. And he was also inclined to be a fighter. Having been baptized at seven months of age in the Catacomb Church, he knew what it meant to fight for what he believed in: "I work now as I have always worked," he was known to remark, "with my face into the wind."

Yakunin would become a fighter, too. He and Men were contemporaries, born only a year apart, and both chose to enter the priesthood. Yakunin graduated from the Moscow Theological Seminary in 1959 and three years later was ordained a priest, assigned to a parish church near Moscow. It wasn't long before he was making his views known — and the Soviet leadership didn't like what it was hearing.

In 1965, Yakunin and fellow priest Nikolai Eschliman wrote an open letter to the patriarch of Moscow arguing that the church be freed from control of the Soviet government. A year later, Yakunin was removed from the parish to which he had been assigned and forbidden to continue ministering there. But the move failed to silence him. A decade later, he formed the Christian Committee for the Defense of the Rights of Believers in the USSR, which promoted religious liberty and highlighted the Soviet government's overbearing restrictions.

It was only a matter of time — and the proper circumstances — before the authorities muzzled him. Their opportunity came in 1979, when Yakunin was taken into custody as part of a sweep that jailed several outspoken Christians. An exiled dissident, Alexander Ginzburg, conjectured that Yakunin had been arrested as part of a campaign to rid Moscow of "undesirable elements" in advance of the Olympic Games (which the city was hosting that year). Or perhaps, he said, it was because they sought to silence any criticism of the Soviet invasion of Afghanistan.

Whatever the reason, he was taken to Lefertovo Prison in the capital and held there for seven months awaiting trial, during which time he had no contact with his wife or anyone else in the outside world. When he finally received his day in court, the judge deemed much of his defense deemed "irrelevant" and refused to allow the testimony of several witnesses before finding him guilty of "anti-Soviet agitation and propaganda."

His sentence: five years in a labor camp and five additional years in exile. As it turned out, he was held at Lefertovo until 1985 before being sent to the Perm 37 labor camp and, subsequently, resettled involuntarily in Yakutia. The sprawling region that takes in much of Siberia lies well to the north of Manchuria, some 3,000 miles from the capital.

"I thank God for this test he has sent me," Yakunin said. "I consider it a great honor and, as a Christian, accept it gladly."

50 UNDEFEATED

Soviet leader Mikhail Gorbachev commuted Yakunin's sentence in 1987, and he was allowed to return to Moscow, where he resumed the priesthood. He undertook a new occupation, as well: 1990 saw his election to the Supreme Soviet of the Russian Federation. The year, however, was noteworthy for a more tragic development, as well. In September, an axe-wielding assailant attacked and murdered Alexander Men as he walked from his home to the train platform in Semkhoz. The crime was committed as he made his way to celebrate the liturgy at his parish, where he had served for more than two decades.

Over the course of the next decade, Yakunin would continue to serve in various Russian parliaments as the nation transitioned from Soviet rule to a new government. In 1992, he led a parliamentary committee that examined the archives of the notorious Soviet spy agency, the KGB. What he found there was reams of evidence that the Orthodox Church had served as a lackey for Soviet leaders.

"It's quite clear that you could not be named a leader without being a signed-up KGB agent, he later said. "They would not allow anyone to go abroad and represent religious organizations without it being controlled by the KGB."

Yakunin had long been suspicious of the church's position as beholden to the government for its existence — that it was, as Yakunin would later describe it, "practically a subsidiary, a sister company of the KGB." And despite the fall of communism, little appeared to have changed. The Soviet system was gone, but the attitude of a church subjugated by and dependent upon the government persisted.

Many sins of the fathers, committed on behalf of the Kremlin, had been swept under the rug for the sake of maintaining the church's reputation.

Yakunin was having none of it. In May of 1996, he accused senior officials within the church of having collaborated with the KGB in the past and of attempting to obscure the fact in the here and now. Referring to documents that came to light during the church's attempt to acquire property in Estonia, Yakunin challenged the church's patriarch to come clean about their contents and the church's ties to Soviet-era spying.

"The tragedy of the church is that after the fall of the antireligious totalitarian system, in six years of complete freedom from state control under your leadership the church still has not been able to move onto the path of spiritual regeneration ...," he wrote. "If Your Supreme Holiness is incapable of ... Christian repentance, then there remains for you only one acceptable course: summon up the courage to retire."

It was a scathing indictment, and one that the church would not allow to go unanswered.

Within the year, Yakunin had been excommunicated.

But not silenced.

He has continued his activities as an activist for human rights and religious freedom, despite the continuing disapproval of a church that remained closely aligned with the Russian government. Most recently, he was heard defending a musical group called Pussy Riot, whose members staged a brief "punk prayer" inside a Moscow cathedral that called on the Virgin Mary to literally chase Russian President Vladimir Putin away.

For their 30-second performance, three of the band members were arrested. They were put behind bars and held for several months awaiting trial, charged with "hooliganism performed by an organized group of people motivated by religious hatred or hostility." The full indictment against them stretched on to an astonishing 2,800 pages.

When they finally got their day in court, the three were convicted. Each was sentenced to two years in custody, and although one was later freed on appeal, the other two found themselves headed to prison camps. (One was bound for a camp in Perm, the same area where Yakunin had been imprisoned for a time nearly three decades earlier.)

Yakunin, meanwhile, asserted that the arrests weren't about hooliganism at all, but rather about daring to oppose the government … and that the church remained, two decades after the fall of the Soviet Union, a creature of those who held political power. In this case, President Putin.

Patriarch Kirill, meanwhile, was at the forefront of those condemning the band's performance, labeling it blasphemous and declaring that "the devil has laughed at all of us." It was a predictable response, considering that Kirill was an enthusiastic supporter of Putin's who had called him no less than a "miracle from God."

"We have no future if we allow mockery in front of great shrines," he said.

Putin, meanwhile, invoked the specter of Soviet rule in justifying the verdict, referring to the huge number of priests who had suffered under Soviet rule.

He might have consulted Yakunin, a defender of Pussy Riot who was, ironically, one of those priests. Here was a man who had, after all, gone to prison for arguing *against* Soviet subjugation of the church. But of course, Putin was invoking Soviet-era policies to justify his own, using the church as a means of maintaining political power.

"When Hitler and Stalin created their powerful, totalitarian regimes, they made use of powerful ideologies," Yakunin said. "Putin seems to be a good administrator, but a weak ideologist, so he decided to use something that already exists."

That something was the church.

It might seem, in light of the sentence passed against Pussy Riot, that not much has changed in Russia. Church and state still conspire against free expression. Christianity is still held in thrall to the church, which in turn is subservient to the government. Those who dare to speak out are still excommunicated, sent to labor camps or otherwise silenced.

Yet because of people like Gleb Yakunin, the fight continues, and progress — in small steps — is being made. The Pussy Riot performance at the Christ the Savior Cathedral was videotaped and went viral on YouTube, where the band found supporters ranging from chess champion Gary Kasparov to pop stars Sting and Madonna. And a new generation of Christians is rising up to carry on the fight, as well. Among them is Sergei Baranov, a deacon in the Orthodox Church who voiced his support for the band members — then tendered his resignation in protest for the church's stance against them.

"Everyone prays as they can," said Baranov. "And with their act they exposed the ills and blisters of society. We should have done that a long time ago."

Gleb Yakunin has been doing it for decades.

Now others are carrying on his work.

And they, like he, will not be silenced.

"The evil genius that created the power of the Soviets… has not yet been completely defeated."

— Gleb Yakunin

STEPHEN H. PROVOST

Emily Edmonson

Daughter of the Pearl

Emily Edmonson may not be as well-known in the annals of the struggle against slavery as Frederick Douglass or Harriet Beecher Stowe. But she has a profound effect on each of them, and something she did while still a child helped set the stage for the eventual emancipation of African-American slaves in the United States.

Edmonson was just 13 years old when she and her older sister, 15-year-old Mary, joined four of their brothers in an audacious attempt to escape a life of slavery for freedom aboard a ship called the Pearl. In all, 77 slaves took part in the largest escape attempt ever made in the United States.

The Edmonson family lived on the cusp of freedom in more ways than one. Maryland, where they made their home, was on the northernmost fringe of the Southern slave states: Pennsylvania, just across the state line, was a free state, and three-quarters of the blacks in the District of Columbia were not under the yoke of slavery.

Many African-Americans in Maryland were free, as well. Indeed, Paul Edmonson — Emily's father — was among them. He owned and farmed his own land; he married and raised a family. His children, however, were born into slavery because their mother was a slave. That was the law.

By the time of the Pearl incident, in 1848, four of the Edmonson children had purchased their freedom. But Emily and Mary weren't given the same opportunity, because their "owner" wouldn't allow it. He wanted to keep them in thrall so he could hire them out as servants to wealthy homeowners — and take the profits for himself.

The situation was, clearly, intolerable. So as night fell on April 15, 1848, the six Edmonson children who remained in slavery resolved to change their fortunes. They ventured forth covertly on that rainy evening to the Potomac River, where a schooner called the Pearl was waiting.

The plan was for the Pearl to travel down the river to Chesapeake Bay, then north through the bay to and east across the Delaware Canal to the free state of New Jersey. Initially, only a handful of slaves signed up to make the attempt, but the word had quickly spread, and their numbers had swollen to nearly four score.

It was nearly midnight by the time the schooner got under way, but they hadn't made it a mile yet when the wind suddenly died, leaving them virtually stranded on the water. It didn't pick up again until morning, giving the slaveholders from whom they'd escaped time to notice they were missing.

They quickly formed a search party to go looking for their missing "property" (valued at something like $100,000), but the ship might still have escaped had the weather not taken another nasty turn. A squall forced the crew to make a difficult choice: drop anchor and wait out the storm or try their luck on the open sea.

The decision was made by a single person: the captain. Edward Sayres was unwilling to risk taking the schooner out onto the open water, so they stayed put, dropping anchor in a small cove and hoping a break in the weather that would allow them to get under way again before they were discovered.

As it turned out, this was too much to hope for. A series of events led the search party to the schooner, and after a brief scuffle, the posse boarded the ship and the slaves surrendered. The worst, however, still lay ahead. An angry mob of about 1,000 agitators showed up outside the offices of an abolitionist newspaper many held responsible for the Pearl incident. Three days of rioting ensued, and the Edmonson children were taken to Baltimore, where they were confined to a slave pen.

Despite the rioting and violence, more rational men and women fought for the slaves' freedom. The Edmonsons' parents tried to raise the money needed to buy their freedom, and in the halls of Congress, Rep. Joshua Giddings of Ohio compared the slaves' quest for freedom with that of the nation's founders. Giddings, who would go on to help form the Republican Party, stated bluntly that an individual who sought to deprive another human being of his freedom did so at his own peril.

Rep. William Haskell of Tennessee responded that Giddings "ought to be hanged as high as Haman" — referring to the Persian vizier in the biblical book of Esther.

Meanwhile, the Edmonsons were unable to raise the necessary money to buy their children's freedom by the time the siblings were sent south to New Orleans on a barge and jailed while they awaited sale to new "owners." One day, one of their own siblings showed up at the jail. He himself had been shipped south several years earlier as a slave, but had succeeded in buying his freedom. Now, he arranged for one of his brothers to gain a position (albeit still as a slave) with an Englishman, working as his butler.

The other siblings, however, were quickly sent back to Alexandria, Va., to protect them (or rather the investment they represented) from an outbreak of yellow fever. While they had been gone, their parents — Paul and Amelia — hadn't lost hope of raising enough money to buy their children's freedom. With their return to the Eastern Seaboard, they redoubled their efforts, enlisting the help of a Congregationalist church in Brooklyn led by the Rev. Henry Ward Beecher. With the church's help, they were able to raise the necessary funds before the plague subsided and their children were shipped back to New Orleans.

Beecher was the brother of Harriet Beecher Stowe, who would shortly publish the groundbreaking anti-slavery novel *Uncle Tom's Cabin*. Slaveholders considered the work such a grave threat that they pushed through laws in Maryland, Delaware and the District of Columbia making it illegal for any African-American — slave or free — to possess a copy. Stowe later published a nonfiction companion titled *Key to Uncle Tom's Cabin*, in which she chronicled the Edmonsons' story.

The Beecher family supported the Edmonson sisters as they went off to attend Oberlin College in Ohio, which had opened its doors to women in 1837 and graduated its first African-American seven years later. The city of Oberlin was a key center for abolitionists who used it as a stop on the Underground Railroad.

Emily Edmonson's stay at Oberlin would be brief, however, as she returned to the Washington area less than a year after leaving. Her sister Mary had taken ill with tuberculosis and died, so Emily — by this time 18 — withdrew from school. She didn't, however, abandon her education. Instead, she enrolled in the Normal School for Colored Girls, a prep school for African-American women interested in becoming teachers in Washington.

A woman named Myrtilla Miner had opened the school after moving from Mississippi, where she had been denied permission to teach classes for African-American girls. In Washington, D.C., she received encouragement from Henry Ward Beecher and funding from a philanthropist for the new school, whose enrollment grew from six to 40 in the space of just two months. Beecher Stowe used $1,000 in royalties from *Uncle Tom's Cabin* to help maintain the school. And Johns Hopkins, a wealthy Quaker who supported the abolitionist cause, served on the first board of trustees.

In 1954, Miner found a permanent campus on a three-acre lot that included a house and a barn at the city's outskirts. It was then that Emily enrolled and went to live with her in the house. Despite the efforts of abolitionists like the Beechers and others, opposition to educating young black women remained high — much as it is today among conservative Muslims in Afghanistan. Some people in the city, where slavery was still legal, were willing to use violence in an attempt to fight the school's mission.

Miner later wrote of the conditions that she and Emily endured: "Emily and I lived here alone, unprotected, except by God. The rowdies occasionally stone our house in the evening. Emily and I have been seen practicing shooting with a pistol. (Members of the Edmonson family) have come with a dog."

Emily eventually married Larkin Johnson and moved to the Anacostia neighborhood of Washington, where their neighbors included Frederick Douglass. One of her grandchildren later wrote, "Grandma & Frederick Douglass were like sister and brother — great abolitionists. I sat on his knee in his office in the house that is now a museum in Anacostia where we were born."

Both the Edmonson sisters and Douglass had attended a convention in 1850 to protest the Fugitive Slave Act, which allowed slave owners to arrest slaves that had escaped to the North. Douglass, a former slave himself who had escaped to freedom in 1838, continued to work in the abolitionist cause and earned a reputation as one of the great orators of his day.

Emily Edmonson, meanwhile, lived to the age of about 60. More than a century after her death, in 2010, a bronze sculpture of her and her sister Mary was unveiled near the site of the building where they were once kept as slaves in a holding facility. Today, it is an office building.

The city also designated one of its parks Edmonson Plaza in honor of Emily and her sister Mary.

A letter quoted in Harriet Beecher Stowe's *Key to Uncle Tom's Cabin* recalls the joy surrounding the day when the two girls gained their freedom:

"I have seen the Edmondson (sic) parents, Paul and his wife Milly. I have seen the *free* Edmondsons — mother son and daughter — the very day after the great era of *free life* commenced … smiling a delightful appreciation of joy in the present and hope for the future, thus suddenly and completely unfolded."

"The limits of tyrants are prescribed by the endurance of those whom they oppose."

— Frederick Douglass

STEPHEN H. PROVOST

David Richard Fandanumata
South Pacific Sorrow

Fans of the American television series *Survivor* may know about the island chain of Vanuatu from the 2004 season. They may remember a fellow named Chris Daugherty, a project inspector for the Ohio Department of Transportation who won $1 million for being the final survivor that season.

They probably won't have heard of David Richard Fandanumata, a resident of Vanuatu who has been working on behalf of a different set of survivors.

Real survivors.

To them and their forebears, survival was not a game. It was a very real challenge in the face of men who removed them by force from their homelands and shipped them across the sea to work in the guano mines of Peru, the cotton fields of Fiji or the sugar cane fields of Queensland, Australia.

People from islands all across the South Pacific were being lured aboard ships by the promise of trade, then the doors were shut behind them and they were transported to South America, Australia or elsewhere to work as slaves. The practice, known as "blackbirding," was occurring even as a Civil War was raging that would result in the emancipation of American slaves — and in many cases long afterward. In fact, the Civil War itself created part of the "demand" for slave labor in places like Fiji. Abducted islanders were taken there to pick cotton — a crop previously supplied in large quantities by slaves in the American South but now in short supply due to the war and subsequent end to slavery.

Many were separated from their clans and families, never to see their homes again. Some workers were shipped to Australia, while others were transported to Fiji and forced to work there under three-year contracts. They were supposed to be returned home afterward. Instead, however, many ship captains simply dumped them in Queensland on the southern continent's northeast coast.

In Australia, the Vanuatu people — who had been displaced themselves — were ordered by their captors to, in turn, displace the aboriginal peoples of Australia.

"From our grandfather who came back to Vanuatu from Australia, we heard the tale that our Vanuatu people had been used to kill the aborigines," Fandanumata said. "The blackbirders told them to poison the water, to use clubs and all things (available to them) to move the aborigines and take their land."

Such was the cycle of violence that the blackbirders initiated across the South Pacific.

Vanuatu was not the only island affected. Far from it. Indeed, slave ships called on numerous islands across the South Pacific, from Vanuatu to Samoa to Easter Island. In Pukapuka, the first South Pacific island ever sighted by Europeans, Peruvian slave traders kidnapped 145 men and women, only two of whom ever returned to their homes.

In Rakahanga, a ring of land rimming a large lagoon in the Cook Islands chain, 115 recruits were taken to Peru.

But perhaps the most tragic story involved Rapa Nui, otherwise known as Easter Island — home of the famed giant statues known as moai. At one time home to as many as 15,000 inhabitants, the population had plummeted to just 20 percent of that by the early 18th century. Aggressive deforestation had left the island barren of large trees, which had been used to build sea vessels for the fishing expeditions crucial to the island's economy. With the trees gone, the bird population also declined dramatically.

These catastrophes, however, would be followed by something even worse: the arrival of blackbirding ships around the time of the U.S. Civil War. As residents of the most remote inhabited island on Earth, the people of Rapa Nui hadn't been converted to Christianity, and their indigenous culture remained fully intact.

That was soon to change.

Shortly after the first ship arrived from Peru in the fall of 1862, a second ship made landing and kidnapped more than 150 men to be sold for a price of $300 apiece. Many of them wound up harvesting guano on the Chincha Islands off Peru.

Guano was highly prized as a fertilizer used in agriculture — so much so that it became the foundation of Peru's economy, a commodity sold at high prices to American and European interests. The droppings from cormorants and other seabirds dried quickly on the arid islands, locking in the chemicals used to fertilize the fields.

More raiding ships followed. A fleet of at least eight other ships left the port of Callao for Rapa Nui, intent upon abducting the island's inhabitants and exploiting them as cheap labor. In one case, a raiding party of 80 people succeeded in rounding up more than 200 of the island's residents. They disembarked one morning, many with instructions to stay hidden on the beach while the rest of the crew laid out a selection of mirrors, necklaces and other trinkets to attract the islanders.

When a crowd had gathered and the islanders were bending over or crouching down to inspect these "treasures," the captain fired his revolver in the air as a signal for the ambush to begin. The raiders who had stayed hidden emerged to capture the unsuspecting islanders, who had been thrown into a panic by the gunfire. On subsequent raids, others met a similar fate — more than 1,400 in all.

In less than a year, more than one-third of Rapa Nui's population had been abducted to work in Peru, including many in the noble and learned class. Even the king and many of his family members were taken. Some were eventually allowed to return, but they brought with them the smallpox virus, which killed off about 1,000 of those who had remained behind.

When all was said and done, nearly 60 percent of the island's population had perished, the socio-cultural system had been devastated and the economy was nonexistent. In 1862, when the first ship arrived, there hadn't been a single Christian on the island; six years later, everyone there had been converted. The king died in Peru, though his 6-year-old son and heir survived the ordeal. Six years later, however, he too was dead.

Of the 1,407 people taken from the island by slave traders, all but one were dead by 1886.

Meanwhile, blackbirders based in Australia continued their raids unabated over a period of four decades. In all, some 62,000 South Pacific islanders wound up in Queensland. Nearly 40,000 came from Vanuatu and 17,000 more from the Solomon Islands. But after the imported laborers had done their dirty work for them, the government of the commonwealth turned the tables and ordered them all deported at the beginning of the 20th century under the so-called White Australia Policy.

In effect, families were separated twice: first when they were uprooted from their home islands, then when they were deported by the Australians — separating them from wives and children. At the end of the 20th century, several thousand descendants of the abducted workers still lived in Queensland.

"Our great grandfather was married to an aborigine in Australia but left behind his wife when he was deported," Fandanumata recalled. "They had a son, but we haven't been able to find him.

"At the time of the White Australia Policy, many of us were sent back to Vanuatu, but some were displaced to other countries or islands or villages, so many of us who are concerned about this issue are related to these lost sons, like some Solomon Islanders or men from Malekula who were left on Tonga Island."

Thanks to the efforts of Fandanumata and others, some healing has begun. The Vanuatu themselves have apologized for their role in killing aboriginal Australians at the behest of the blackbirders. "We were happy for this story to come out, so we could say 'sorry' on behalf of the Pacific," Fandanumata said. "That's the custom of the Pacific — if we go to someone else's place, we must say 'sorry' for wrongs."

Apologies came (if belatedly) from Australia, as well. It wasn't until the dawn of the new millennium, on Sept. 7, 2000, that the government of Queensland recognized South Sea Islander Australians as a unique ethic group. Eight years later, the government issued a formal apology to the indigenous South Sea peoples displaced by the blackbird slave ships.

In the summer of 2012, Fandanumata visited the sites along the northeastern coast of Australia where men and women from his island were deposited by the blackbirders, bound for work on the sugarcane plantations. In one case, the crew of a blackbirder ship poured scalding water over them and then threw them overboard.

He visited the sites where they once worked in the cane fields and saw pieces of wood from the first church where the laborers congregated and the graveyard where they are buried. "If you go to their cemetery, you will see customs names from Vanuatu, from different islands, inscribed on the tombstones of our ancestors," the chief said.

Today, efforts are being made to locate and reunite families separated for a century and a half. A website launched in 2003 aimed to reconnect the descendants of family members sent abroad during the blackbirding era. The website announces "the largest Pacific and South Sea Islander genealogical and historical project ever to be conducted."

The site called "Blackbird currently helps with finding and reconnecting families in Australia, Vanuatu and the Solomon Islands, using all means available including ship logs, historical records, oral history and information from the families themselves.'"

The effort is, for obvious reasons, a tall order.

50 UNDEFEATED

"The tragedy is that we do not know what happened to our ancestors who were blackbirded to Australia between 1847 and 1863," Fandanumata explained, "because the information is not available."

Still, for many, there is renewed hope that the story of an unspeakably horrific era in the history of humankind can be brought, at last, to a close.

"In those days, the foundation of Australia's economy grew on the hands, shoulders and backsides of our ancestors."

— Chief David Richard Fandanumata

Jeannette Rankin
Peacemaker

People who stand up for their principles sometimes have to stand out — and stand alone.

Jeannette Rankin made a habit of that.

It was 1917 when she was elected to the U.S. House of Representatives from the state of Montana. Yes, you read that date right. Rankin was elected to Congress three years *before* the 19th Amendment to the U.S. Constitution guaranteed women the right to vote.

Some states, however, had been ahead of the curve. Among them was Montana, where Rankin's efforts as a lobbyist for the American Woman Suffrage Association gave women the right to vote in 1914. Her campaign was tenacious and wide-ranging, as she undertook a barnstorming tour that covered some 5,000 miles in less than six months. Those tireless efforts paid off when the measure allowing women to vote in the state passed by four percentage points.

They paid off for Rankin personally when, two years later, she pursued election to the House from Montana as a Republican. She finished second in the balloting, but because Montana's two House seats were filled on an at-large basis, she secured one of them.

She took office in 1917, bringing with her an agenda that included national suffrage for women, child-protection laws and pacifism — a position that would be put to the test almost immediately on her arrival in Washington.

50 UNDEFEATED

Rankin quickly became caught up in a debate over American involvement in World War I. As a pacifist, she was steadfastly against it, but with President Woodrow Wilson having sought support for the war effort to "make the world safe for democracy," she was in an awkward position.

At the time of her election, the United States was maintaining a clear policy of non-intervention, even after a German U-boat sank the British ocean liner the *Lusitania* in 1915. The following year, Wilson ran on his record of having kept the United States out of the war, putting him firmly in the same camp as Rankin.

But in 1917, things changed. Germany began pursuing an aggressive policy of submarine warfare, sinking seven U.S. merchant ships and subs. This — together with a letter from Germany to Mexico offering its support in annexing Arizona, New Mexico and Texas from the United States — turned the tide of public opinion from isolationism toward war.

Rankin, however, stuck to her principles. Fellow advocates of women's suffrage warned her that a vote against the war could hurt their cause, but this was not a compromise she was willing to make. "I want to stand by my country, but I cannot vote for war," she said. "I vote no."

She was one of only 50 House members to vote against U.S. involvement, and in doing so, she sealed her political fate (at least for the moment). A newspaper in her home state, the Helena Independent, lambasted her as "a dagger in the hands of the German propagandists, a dupe of the Kaiser, a member of the Hun army in the United States, and a crying schoolgirl."

The fears of Rankin's fellow suffragists ultimately proved unfounded. She successfully pushed for the creation of a committee on women's suffrage, of which she then became a member. When debate began on a proposed constitutional amendment, Rankin was the first to speak, even referring back to the war vote in doing so: "How shall we explain … the meaning of democracy if the same

Congress that voted to make the world safe for democracy refuses to give this small measure of democracy to the women of our country?"

The proposed amendment won approval in the House but failed to pass muster in the Senate. Still, it was a start. And two years later, the process that Rankin had helped kick-start in Congress culminated in the passage of the 19th Amendment to the U.S. Constitution, which gave women the right to vote across the entire nation.

Its passage came nearly four years after Rankin's election and, by the time it became the law of the land, she was no longer serving as a representative of Montana. In part, this was due to a change in the voting rules for her home state, which had replaced its two at-large seats with a pair of districts to be voted upon separately. That left Rankin with the unenviable choice of running against an incumbent from her own party in one district or trying to win in the other — which was controlled by Democrats.

Instead, she decided to run for the Senate, losing in the primary by just 2,000 votes and finishing third when she launched a third-party campaign in the general election.

Upon leaving public office, Rankin continued her focus on social issues such as consumer advocacy and the effort to ban child labor. In 1920, she became a founding member of the American Civil Liberties Union. She also continued her involvement in the anti-war movement, forming the Georgia Peace Society in 1928 and serving as a lobbyist for the National Council for the Prevention of War.

Those anti-war convictions led her to consider another run for Congress at the age of 60 in 1940, more than two decades after she was first elected. As before, she made no secret of the fact that she was a pacifist, but she argued for a modern military as a means of preventing war: "By voting for me, you can express your opposition to sending your son to foreign lands to fight in a foreign war," she said. "And by voting for me you will also express your determination to prepare to the absolute limit to defend this country."

On Election Day, Rankin won by more than 9,000 votes, but predicted that "no one will pay any attention to me this time — there is nothing unusual about a woman being elected."

But history was about to repeat itself: Once again, Rankin found herself elected to Congress at a time when the United States was on the brink of war. Wilson had been wrong a quarter-century earlier when he had declared The Great War — which had claimed the lives of 116,000 American soldiers — would "end all wars." Soon, no one would be calling that conflict The Great War, but rather World War I, the change and added numeral rendered necessary by a second and even more catastrophic global war.

As she had in her previous congressional term, Rankin found herself in the minority on the issue. After the attack on Pearl Harbor, she remained resolute in her opposition to sending American soldiers overseas. Her rationale was simple: "As a woman I can't go to war, and I refuse to send anyone else."

But it was also strategic. She recalled what another member of the House had told her after she voted against involvement in the first world war — if he had known in advance that she would oppose it, he might have had the courage to do the same. "I decided then that never would I wait to prepare a speech, that I'd speak out any time, and so when they read the resolution, I asked to have it referred to committee.

"According to the rules of Congress, a resolution, once introduced, has to be referred to a committee if anyone asks for it to be referred to a committee. I hoped that by voting no and refusing unanimity to the vote, and by asking that it be referred to a committee, I could remove the war vote from the passion of the moment and have it considered so both sides of the issues could be brought out."

It didn't work out that way. When she voted against the war resolution, Rankin's announcement was reportedly greeted by "a chorus of hisses and boos." When she had opposed American entry into the first world war, 49 other representatives had voted with her; this time, she stood alone. The final tally was 388-1.

Again, her political fate was sealed.

After a single term, Rankin left office again. She largely retired from public life and stayed out of the limelight, traveling to India seven times, where she studied the work and teachings of Mohandas K. Gandhi. One final time, in the late 1960s, she became involved publicly in politics — as an opponent to the Vietnam War. On Jan. 15, 1968, at the age of 87, she organized 5,000 protesters for a march on Washington to demand peace. When asked if she was advocating surrender, she replied, "Surrender is a military idea. When you're doing something wrong, you stop."

At the time of her death in 1973, just shy of her 93rd birthday, she was considering yet another run for Congress on an anti-war platform. She bequeathed her property to help "mature, unemployed women workers," a gift that laid the groundwork for the Jeanette Rankin Foundation. Its mission: to award educational scholarships to low-income women.

Many have criticized Rankin's anti-war stands, particularly her lone vote against joining World War II, but her place in American history as a key proponent of women's, children's and civil rights is secure. And whatever anyone's ultimate judgment of her anti-war crusades may be, it can at least be said that she stood by her principles.

"I voted my convictions and my campaign pledges," she said of her World War II dissent. "I have nothing left but my integrity."

That's far more than most politicians can say.

"What one decides to do in crisis depends on one's philosophy, and that philosophy cannot be changed by an incident. If one hasn't any philosophy in crises, others make the decision."

— Jeannette Rankin

Wally Yonamine
Man in the Middle

Wally Yonamine was born in Hawaii, halfway between two worlds on the island of Maui. To the west lay his parents' homeland, Japan; to the east was the U.S. mainland. Hawaii itself wasn't a state yet, but a territory, and it wasn't the tourist destination it is now.

"It was an extremely beautiful, quiet, small place when I was a kid," Yonamine would recall. "No one came there then. In those days, you didn't see a single face in (the town of) Lahaina you didn't know."

Yonamine grew up listening to baseball on the radio. But football was the big game on the islands. High school games at Honolulu Stadium on Oahu were major events, with thousands of people turning out to watch the boys play. He soon would get his chance to join them.

The year was 1941 when Yonamine entered ninth grade at Lahainaluna School in Lahaina, the oldest American-run school west of the Rockies. He had never played a single down of organized football, but he made the team anyway and settled into his expected role as a benchwarmer.

But not for long.

In the first quarter of the season's very first game, the freshman got his chance to make an impression when the starting halfback broke his thumb.

50 UNDEFEATED

He made the most of it. On the first play from scrimmage, the quarterback tossed him the ball and he threw it toward the end zone. Thirty-five yards later, the receiver caught it for a touchdown. Later in the game, he ran 11 yards for another score, and in the final quarter — playing defense with the opposing team driving — he stepped in front of a pass and returned it 70 yards for a touchdown. He accounted for all three touchdowns in a 19-7 victory that produced a glowing headline the next day in the *Maui News*: "Yonamine Leads Lunas to 19-7 Win."

Yonamine remained the starting halfback for the rest of the season, helping Lahainaluna to the Maui championship and a berth in the Haleakala Bowl against the champions of the chain's most populous island, Oahu. His team lost that game, and a week later, the Japanese bombed Pearl Harbor.

Unlike Japanese Americans in the western U.S. mainland, Yonamine and his family weren't forced into a relocation camp — Japanese Americans in Hawaii weren't subject to that indignity — but he still faced discrimination. Japanese Hawaiians were subject to racial slurs and other forms of prejudice; some employers wouldn't hire them, and hundreds of community leaders were even arrested. Even in this atmosphere, however, Yonamine was able to continue his football career, earning Maui all-star honors as a sophomore and helping Lahainaluna win another island championship.

A year later, he transferred to a school on Oahu, where he excelled before entering the military. Drafted in 1944, he entered basic training but never saw action, as the Japanese surrendered a month and a half later. He continued to play football in the Army, however, and also played some baseball against touring major leaguers such as Stan Musial and Joe DiMaggio.

Upon his discharge, he joined an amateur football team in Hawaii.

At the time, a new professional football league was being formed to compete with the NFL. The All-America Football Conference would last four years, and two of its teams — the San Francisco

49ers and Cleveland Browns — would end up as long-term members of the NFL after a merger. But in 1947, a year after the league formed, its teams were still was on the lookout for players with talent who might have been overlooked by the more established league.

Yonamine had just that kind of talent. While barnstorming in Oregon with a team called the Hawaiian Warriors, he caught the eye of professional scouts. It wasn't long before he signed a two-year, $14,000 contract with the San Francisco 49ers, becoming the first person of Asian ancestry to play professional football. But like Jackie Robinson, who started out as a star football player and later made his name in a different sport, Yonamine's fame wouldn't be based on his gridiron prowess.

He played only one season with the 49ers, starting three of the team's 12 games and rushing for 74 yards on 19 carries. He also caught three passes for 40 yards more and played on special teams, providing a key punt return against Buffalo that ignited a 34-point outburst in a 41-24 victory.

But like Robinson, who broke into the majors the same year Yonamine debuted with the 49ers, it was an injury that spelled the end of his career. His contract stated he had to be physically fit by the time training camp started in 1948, and he wasn't, so the team released him.

Yonamine never played the second season on that two-year contract because he broke his wrist during the offseason playing a different sport, baseball.

And it was in baseball that he, like Robinson, would make his name.

"I tell people it must have been the Lord's plan for me to play baseball," he said. "Everything turned out for the best."

As a youth, Yonamine had spent his summers growing up working on a plantation, using a machete to cut sugarcane stalks. "I used to really hate that job," he said. "I got paid only twenty-five cents a day, but it was the only job I could get. At the time, I told myself that I never wanted to work in the cane fields again."

He wouldn't have to. When the 49ers released the injured halfback after his first season, he started swinging something other than a machete much more often — a baseball bat. Yomamine got in touch with Lefty O'Doul, a two-time National League batting champion who had become manager of the San Francisco Seals in the Pacific Coast League.

"I had met Lefty O'Doul in Hawaii when he brought some major league all-stars over there during the war," Yonamine said. "He liked the way I played. So after I got hurt with the 49ers, I contacted him."

The Seals signed him to a contract, and in 1950, O'Doul sent him to their farm team in Salt Lake City, the Bees, where he hit .335 (fourth-best in the league) while playing outfield and first base.

He was a natural choice to be called up to the Seals, but O'Doul had a different idea. Cappy Harada, a Japanese American from Santa Maria, California, had been inspired to use baseball as a means of repairing some of the damage done by the war. He arranged goodwill tours of Japan featuring American baseball players such as Joe DiMaggio, and O'Doul's Seals participated in one such event in 1949. At some point, the idea arose of having Yonamine play in Japan. He would become the first American to play baseball there since the war — becoming a trailblazer in the mold of Jackie Robinson.

"I was the No. 4 hitter in the league (with Salt Lake City), but I wasn't hitting home runs, and I knew that would keep me out of the majors," Yonamine said. "So Lefty suggested I take a crack at Japanese ball. I owe him a lot."

Like Robinson, however, Yonamine faced plenty of obstacles.

For one thing, he spoke very little Japanese. For another, his more aggressive style of baseball, in which he would slide hard into second base to break up a double play, didn't go over well initially in the more gentlemanly Japanese game. But more than anything else, being an American made him a target for discrimination.

"Although I had it rough, Jackie Robinson had it much rougher," he said. "You see, my skin is yellow just like the Japanese."

Perhaps.

Or maybe Yonamine was downplaying the challenge just a little. This was the same star athlete who once objected to signing his autograph after scoring all his team's points in a high school football game, saying, "I'm no big shot."

In fact, he was subjected to constant heckling from Japanese who shouted out, "Hawaii e kaere!" (translation: "Go back to Hawaii!"). Fans in Osaka threw rocks at him, gangsters in Hiroshima threatened his life, and a mob of fans in Nagoya chased him into the dugout. Through all this, however, he emerged as a bona fide star, finishing his rookie season with a .354 average as his team — the Yomiuri Giants — won the first of eight pennants during his tenure.

Two years later, he did even better, winning the first of three batting titles with a .361 average as he led the league in runs, hits and doubles. He won two more batting championships in 1956 and '57, moving to the Chunichi Dragons for his final two seasons before retiring in 1962.

Ten years later, he became the team's manager and led them to a pennant in his third season. The victory was especially sweet, as it came against his other former team, Yomiuri, which had won nine consecutive championships.

In 1994, Yonamine was elected to the Japanese Baseball Hall of Fame. The same man who once tried to politely decline autograph seekers had become famous enough to sign his name for no less a figure as Sadaharu Oh, who would go on to hit more home runs than any other professional player in history.

"The first autograph I got was from Mr. Yonamine," Oh said. "He taught me about the game of baseball when I entered the pro league, and he was like my mentor."

Yonamine, who later became a scout in Japan, didn't forget his roots in Hawaii. He started a foundation that, in 1997, began sponsoring the state's annual baseball tournament. Nine years later, it created a $200,000 endowment to ensure the event would continue.

Yonamine died in 2011, having achieved all he set out to accomplish.

50 UNDEFEATED

"When I came to Japan, I wanted to do three things: to manage a championship team, get into the Hall of Fame and to shake hands with the emperor," he said. He succeeded in the first two, but meeting the emperor? That seemed out of the question.

"I thought meeting the emperor would be impossible," he related. "But when I was a scout with the Giants, my wife and I met the emperor and the empress in Los Angeles. ... As they were walking out of the room, the empress looked at me and took a practice swing. There she was, the *empress* in the nice kimono and all that, giving me this batting stance!"

"I went through hell that first year (in Japan). I knew I had to make them change their minds for the others after me as well as myself."

— Wally Yonamine

Kalpana Saroj
Caste Aside

In India, they're called untouchables. The Dalits represent 16 percent of the country's population, and many of its citizens want nothing to do with them. They're shunned, dismissed and relegated to the lowest rung of the social and economic ladder. What's worse, is they can't rise above it.

India's constitution outlaws discrimination against Dalits, a word that means "broken" or "suppressed." But just as prejudice continued after the formal abolition of slavery in the United States, it has continued under India's caste system. Historically, the untouchables have been manual laborers who exposed themselves to ritual impurity by handling animal skins, cleaning waste products and removing trash.

If you are born into this group, that's the kind of work you will do. You can't marry outside your caste, within which you grow up, marry, grow old and die. No matter what you do, your caste doesn't change.

Kalpana Saroj challenged this.

Born a Dalit, she was barred from entering some of her friends' homes during childhood — a childhood that didn't last long. By the age of 12, she had been married to a man a decade her senior and taken from her village to a new life in Mumbai. If you could call it that. Her new in-laws, she said, "would pull my hair and beat me, sometimes over little things." Her brother-in-law was an alcoholic and demanded to know whom her mother had slept with to produce "this donkey." She lost weight and was given only torn clothes to wear.

She said she felt broken — the very meaning of the word Dalit — but was able to escape the abuse in Mumbai thanks to her father, who came to visit her and was appalled at how she was being treated. She was not, however, able to escape being a Dalit. There was no escape from that.

Saroj learned the craft of tailoring and started to make money, but she was so despondent that she decided there was no point in living any longer. "One day," she said, "I decided to end my life. I drank three bottles of insecticide — termite poisoning." Her aunt, however, walked in on her and found her in convulsions, foaming at the mouth. Though Saroj fell into a coma, she survived.

But her own health problems weren't the catalyst that changed her life. When her sister died because she couldn't afford to go to the hospital, Saroj realized that, "if it's all about money, I need to control it." So she borrowed $1,000 under a government program and opened a business making clothing and furniture. She got a good price on a piece of property and purchased it.

Her business did well, and she invested in a sugar company and a maker of industrial equipment that was struggling. Saroj restructured it and turned it around, erasing a mound of debt and turning it into a company worth more than $100 million that employs hundreds. She has remarried and has two children. One daughter began studying hotel management, so Saroj bought her a hotel.

She's not the only Dalit to improve her lot. In 2009, Meira Kumar became the first Dalit woman to serve as speaker of the Indian Parliament. But the odds remain stacked heavily against the untouchables.

"It's impossible for the poor, minorities and low castes to get justice," said Udit Raj, a Dalit leader who called Kumar's election a symbolic victory. "There is some way to go before Dalits get the respect they're entitled to under the constitution."

Indeed.

Two years before Kumar's election, the poverty rate among Dalits stood at 39 percent, compared to 27 percent for the nation as a whole.

According to a Human Rights Watch survey conducted that same year, Dalits remained segregated from other children in nearly four out of every ten schools, and nearly two-thirds of all villages prohibited them from entering temples. One-third of public health workers refused to enter a Dalit home, and the vast majority of villages did not allow Dalits to eat alongside others.

None of that, however, can detract from Saroj's success story.

"I'm aware people may still look down on me because I'm a Dalit," she said, "but even when I was very agitated, I never lost my cool, always trying instead to find my way out of difficult situations."

"I was treated as something lower than a person, but I'll die a human being."

— Kalpana Saroj

Sam Clemens
Put It On My Tab

Imagine off-roading it across the western half of the North American continent.

Without an engine.

Our hero managed to endure that trial, but he faced a great many more. He dealt with a drinking habit that left him continually wanting for cash. As a prospector, he allowed a rich claim — and a fortune in gold — to slip through his fingers through a combination of charity and carelessness. He was challenged to a duel (twice) and run out of town. And he was, by his own admission, a "slouch" of a public speaker who spoke so softly his first audience couldn't even hear him.

He did some writing, but he was invited to contribute one of his stories for an anthology being published by a famous friend, he procrastinated so long that the book came out before the story was even finished.

He went west to escape the Civil War, and began his often-sidetracked journey to success by crossing a desert so dry and barren that it was littered with the bones of animals... and humans. The Donner Pass had nothing on the 40-Mile Desert, a godforsaken stretch of sand and salt flats in what today is northern Nevada.

"From one extremity of this desert to the other," he remarked, the path "was white with the bones of oxen and horses. It would hardly be an exaggeration to say that we could have walked the forty miles and set our feet on a bone at every step!"

This intrepid pioneer survived to reach his destination, but that was far from the end of the challenges he faced.

He and a friend tried their hands at logging near Lake Tahoe, but they spent more time drinking, playing cards, and goofing off than felling trees. (They cut down a grand total of three, which they used to stake their claim to a piece of land.) They tried to fish but didn't catch much. Then they "borrowed" a boat and supplies from a nearby camp when its occupants were away, but the entire enterprise blew up in their faces when they had to flee after accidentally starting a forest fire.

Logging clearly wasn't his cup of tea, so he tried mining for gold instead..

Going back in the direction he had come, he endured a snowstorm and bitter cold to set up a crude cabin in the boomtown of Unionville — which wasn't nearly as impressive as his name. By his account, it consisted of nothing more than "eleven cabins and a liberty-pole." It would have been nice to say he beat the odds and struck it rich in Unionville, but sadly, his search for silver there came up empty.

Not to be discouraged, he tried again, heading back west to the next big boomtown: Aurora. He had better luck there, landing a mill job that paid him $10 a week and staking a claim so rich that, in his words, it made him and his partner "millionaires for 10 days."

He never saw a dime of it, though. When he left town abruptly to visit and care for a friend who had fallen ill, he returned to find several gun-toting "gentlemen" had jumped his claim. It was all perfectly legal, it turned out: Under a local ordinance, a claim became null and void once it had been left untended for 10 days. Those 10 days had elapsed, and the claim was, therefore, forfeit.

Still undeterred, the disappointed prospector turned to writing, landing a job at Nevada's biggest newspaper: the *Territorial Enterprise* in Virginia City. He wasn't the star reporter there (a friend and colleague by the nom de plume of Dan De Quille built a bigger reputation). And he spent a lot of his off hours getting drunk at various local saloons, typically ordering a second drink before he'd paid for the first.

Our friend also tried public speaking, but "didn't talk loud enough," although he received a gold watch for his efforts, despite being, in his own estimation, "an oratorical slouch."

He did well enough to be named editor for a week — but so greatly offended a ladies' aid group with one of his columns that the group expelled his sister-in-law and its president challenged him to a duel. He also offended a rival newspaper's editor, who (you guessed it) challenged him to another duel.

Faced with such animosity, he did the only sensible thing: He abandoned his career as a journalist and left town.

To his credit, he didn't stop writing.

Invited to submit a story for an anthology, he put things off so long that the deadline passed and the book was printed before he sent it off. Fortunately, the publisher suggested that he submit it instead to the *New York Sunday Press*, where it was such a hit that "Jim Smiley and His Jumping Frog" was syndicated.

Later retitled "The Celebrated Jumping Frog of Calaveras County," it kickstarted the career of arguably America's most famous author. Samuel Clemens became quite the orator, too, entertaining audiences across the country with his tales (tall and otherwise).

He retitled himself, as well, becoming known as Mark Twain. Some say he was inspired by his earlier life on the Mississippi River. But Nevada residents point to his saloon days in Virginia City, where he declined to pay for that first drink before ordering a second. He'd instruct the barkeep to put a second (twain) mark next to his name on the board behind the bar.

Instead of "put it on my tab," he just said, "mark twain!"

"Books are the liberated spirits of men."

— Mark Twain

STEPHEN H. PROVOST

Lhakpa Tsering
Don't Try This at Home

These days, Lhakpa Tsering is an actor and a director in Dharmshala, India, but in 2006, he was engaged in a different kind of performance — one that caught the attention of media outlets around the world and more importantly, the Chinese president.

Many terms could have been used to describe what Tsering did outside the Taj Hotel in Mumbai on November 23 of that year. Insane. Radical. Courageous. Desperate. Or maybe just determined. However you describe it, Tsering made a statement.

Having purchased a liter of kerosene at a gas station earlier in the day, Tsering and six other young Tibetans arrived at the hotel in taxis while Chinese President Hu Jintao was inside schmoozing with Indian business leaders. The occasion was the India-China Economic, Trade and Investment Cooperation Summit.

Tsering and the six who arrived with him had no interest in cooperation. The youths unfurled "Free Tibet" banners and tossed a thick stack of papers into the air — letters addressed to Hu — before Tsering doused the legs of his trousers in kerosene and lit them ablaze.

Then, he ran forward, shouting, "Free Tibet!" and "Hu Jintao is the killer! He killed our people!"

Tsering had come a long way from being a 9-year-old boy intent on fleeing Tibet — not to escape political repression, but an abusive home. Born in the summer of 1983 in the village of Tsona near

Tibet's border with India, his childhood was far from ideal. He was sent to boarding school in the first grade, only to be pulled out because his father insisted that the young boy help him watch over a herd of yaks. Waking him while it was still pitch black outside, the man would force his young stepson to wash dirty clothes in the icy river waters thousands of feet up in the Himalayas. When his mother tried to intervene, he took burning sticks from the fire and beat her with them.

It was then that Tsering, feeling he was to blame for his mother's treatment, resolved to leave for India.

He would never see her again.

Setting out during monsoon season, he made it across the border despite nearly drowning in a swollen river and hiding from a pack of wild dogs. Traveling without a passport or any money, the first person he happened to meet was, fortunately, another refugee. Like Tsering, the man had escaped Tibet — but years earlier. After refusing the man's entreaties to return, he was taken to a police camp and sent from there to meet a delegation representing the Dalai Lama.

In short order, he was taken to a boarding school for refugee children from Tibet… and was amazed to find he wasn't the only one who had crossed the border. Two thousand other children at the school had done the same.

Tsering learned the others hadn't left to escape abusive families but the oppressive government of China, which claimed Tibet as part of its territory. Indeed, about 130,000 Tibetan exiles had escaped to India, having fled a regime intent on restraining their freedom.

The Chinese Army had entered Tibet in 1950 and asserted sovereignty over the region. The communist government of Mao Zedong then forced a 17-point agreement that Tibet's leader, the Dalai Lama, repudiated as having been "thrust upon the Tibetan government by threat of arms."

The Dalai Lama himself was forced to flee the country in 1959, and many others followed. The repression, meanwhile, continued.

Three decades later, in 1989, the Chinese government ordered a crackdown on peaceful demonstrations that led to the deaths of 450 Tibetans. The person in charge of that crackdown was none other than Hu Jintao, who had been transferred to Tibet a year earlier and would become China's president in 2003.

Learning of the incident helped cement Tsering's anger toward Hu: "He is the butcher of Tibet," he would say simply in an interview with Lea Thau. "I see him as a rat."

Tsering eventually decided to pursue a master's degree at St. Joseph College in Bangalore and became regional director of the Tibetan Youth Congress. He didn't initially intend to light himself on fire in Mumbai. Not at all. In fact, he and fellow students had been planning a massive demonstration for Bangalore — Hu's original destination — before the president's itinerary was changed at the last minute ... not doubt to forestall protests just like the one Tsering and his cohorts had been planning.

Unable to reschedule a large-scale protest on short notice, Tsering and a few others headed for Mumbai and improvised. Tsering later said he had no intention of becoming a martyr, but felt like he needed to do something dramatic to call attention to the Chinese crimes against the Tibetan people.

As it turned out, he survived the ordeal. Police jumped on him and rolled him on the ground, quickly dousing the flames before rushing him to a hospital. China's government responded officially to the protests with a terse statement that "Tibet is part of China" according to a "widely recognized consensus of the international community." But China was clearly rattled: Hu canceled his remaining scheduled stops in India and returned home.

Tsering eventually recovered from his injuries but lived in some pain thereafter, undergoing surgery in 2011. Still, he had no regrets. "The pain is nothing compared to what Tibetans have put up with under the Chinese regime," he said.

A meeting with the Dalai Lama — whose government in exile had its headquarters in India — followed, and Tsering remained active in the Tibetan Youth Congress but eventually turned his attention to theater, co-founding the Tibet Theatre, "an indigenous and alternative theatre played in Tibetan, reflecting the foibles and triumphs of the exile community, relying largely on satire and comedy."

Tsering's methods may have changed, but his goal of preserving Tibetan culture and advocating for Tibetan freedom are the same.

"We're very excited about Tibet Theatre because it is completely different from traditional Tibetan theatre, which focuses on ancient stories through opera," he said in announcing the theatre's opening.

"In modern-day Tibetan society, we're facing social problems such as the growing generation gap, and the danger of our culture and traditions dying out. In history, theatre has played an important part in influencing revolutions in people's minds. I hope that Tibet Theatre will help people to take more responsibilities within our society."

Its first performance was set for July 6, 2011, the Dalai Lama's 76th birthday.

"We want to draw the world's attention to the lack of freedom and human rights in Tibet. We have had many protests in Bangalore, but this was the time and place where we could make ourselves heard."

— Lhakpa Tsering

Susan Butcher
Breaking the Ice

Susan Butcher wasn't the first woman to win the Iditarod dog sled race or even the first to compete, but she was the first woman — and just the second musher overall — to win it four times. Yet even so, she had to overcome a persistent prejudice that only added to the challenge of covering roughly 1,000 miles across Alaska in some of the harshest conditions imaginable.

Indeed, to call the Iditarod a challenge is a vast understatement. Mushers use sleds of 12-16 dogs to cover one of two routes that wind through Alaska's interior in late winter — hardly the most favorable time to travel across the arctic landscape.

You know that old saying about the U.S. Postal Service delivering the mail regardless of the conditions? Well, the mail carriers have nothing on the participants in what is sometimes called "the last great race on Earth."

It began in 1973 as a tribute to efforts by dog sled teams to transport critically needed medicine from Nenana to Nome, where an outbreak of diphtheria threatened the population a half-century earlier. Balto, a Siberian Husky who covered the final leg and delivered the life-saving antitoxin to the remote town, became a hero in the aftermath of what became known as the Great Race of Mercy.

Though their mission was by no means as desperate, Iditarod mushers faced conditions that could be just as harrowing. In 2012, for example, the race went forward despite record snowfall in

Anchorage, where it has its ceremonial start before beginning in earnest to the north in Willow.

"The ideal conditions for the Iditarod will vary depending on the musher," race communications director Fran McClarnon said. "However, I think most agree that adequate snow coverage of approximately 1 foot-plus, plus temperatures that hover around 10 degrees Fahrenheit to minus-20 degrees Fahrenheit are perfect."

McClarnon, however, added this caveat: "It's rare that you find these consistent conditions over 975 miles."

In 1990, for instance, 70 race participants faced what one report described as some of the worst conditions since the first race 17 years earlier. Mushers were met with a wind chill of 60 below zero, gale-force winds, the deepest snow in a quarter-century and ash spewed 45,000 feet into the sky by Redoubt Volcano.

"Nature is throwing everything at us it can," race manager Jack Niggemyer said. "It might slow things down a bit."

Actually, it didn't.

Amazingly, the winner of that race finished in then-record time, covering the course in 11 days, 1 hour, 53 minutes and 23 seconds. That winner was Susan Butcher, who took first place for the fourth and final time in her career.

Butcher was born in 1954 in Cambridge, Mass. She overcame dyslexia in high school and attended Colorado State University and became a veterinary technician. She enjoyed working with animals, but she yearned to be outdoors; that yearning, and her dyslexia, made the classroom a less-than-ideal setting for her.

She realized early on that she was different.

"I couldn't find role models that I liked," she would recall later. "There were people who were adventurers, but … they were all men. … I was frustrated with the lack of female role models as a child, and wondered why I wanted to do so many things that, at the time, weren't very typical for a woman to be doing."

She would soon get her chance to do one of them. In 1973, Butcher moved to the Wrangell Mountains region of Alaska. In an isolated wilderness with no electricity or running water, she said, "I just lived out there in the bush and basically taught myself how to mush for real and how to survive in the wilderness and what to do."

That knowledge came in handy when Butcher decided to pursue competing in the Iditarod. In 1977, she moved to the community of Kantishna, a former gold mining camp 300 miles north of Anchorage once known as Eureka. Two years later, she became the first woman to finish among the race's top 10.

"It never did occur to me that this was something a woman shouldn't do," she said. "There were no competitive women racing at that time in long-distance racing."

Two or three women had taken part in the Iditarod before her, but she didn't just want to participate. She wanted to win — which made her a threat to the men in the race.

"I was astounded and very unhappy my first year when I found that there was some resistance from my fellow mushers because I was a woman," Butcher said. Her philosophy was to ignore the prejudice and move forward despite "the problems and some of the prejudices that were very strong there and knocking me in the face."

Some critics even tried to dismiss her success by claiming that she used performance-enhancing drugs on her dogs. Tests were done, and each time, the dogs passed with flying colors.

"I did not specifically set out to be a pioneer for women. To me, I was always very aware that I was a woman, and I was very aware that I was the only woman being competitive. But I also saw … that I was a human being and that's how I wanted to be accepted. I didn't see why people couldn't accept that right away. But it wasn't until I became accepted as well as I have now that I realize the struggle that I did go through."

That struggle required physical toughness as well for Butcher, who stood 5 feet, 6 inches and weighed 135 pounds. She ran, mushed, lifted weights, skied or swam every day of the year preparing for the race.

50 UNDEFEATED

Butcher might have become the first woman to win the race had she not faced the most harrowing conditions in Iditarod history — and a bit of bad luck — in 1985. That year, the race was suspended for the first time when weather once prevented the delivery of supplies and also forced the race itself to a halt. Butcher, meanwhile, had to withdraw after a pregnant moose attacked her team, killing two of her dogs.

The winner that year was Libby Riddles, who became the first woman to claim the top prize.

But Butcher returned the next year and won it herself, then repeated the feat the following two years. Soon, shops were selling T-shirts that read: "Alaska: Where Men Are Men and Women Win the Iditarod."

Butcher finally retired from racing in 1994 at the age of 39, raising a family and continuing to breed dogs. As a vet tech and animal lover, she dismissed the notion that racing constituted a form of animal cruelty. Racing "is what they live for," she said. "From the time they see the harness come out or see the sled, they are absolutely going crazy, jumping around, wanting to go and then literally jumping into the harness."

Butcher was diagnosed with leukemia in late 2005 and died in August of the following year. Today, Alaska celebrates the first Saturday of every March as Susan Butcher Day.

"I do not know the word 'quit.' Either I never did, or I have abolished it."

— Susan Butcher

Dalton Trumbo
Phantom of the Oscars

Robert Rich wasn't on hand to accept the Oscar for best original story at the Academy Awards in 1956. He wasn't some self-important prima donna who decided to snub the Academy that year. Jesse Lasky Jr. accepted the award on his behalf and gave the excuse that Rich's wife was in the hospital, poised to give birth.

But that wasn't true, either.

The fact of the matter is that Robert Rich was dead — or he might as well have been ... except he was never really alive in the first place.

Because, technically, he didn't exist.

You couldn't really call Rich a ghostwriter, because the person who wrote the screenplay for *The Brave One* was very much alive. It's just that he wasn't named Rich — an ironic name, in a sense, because the man behind that name wasn't making much money at the time. During one two-year stretch, he was earning an average of just $1,750 for 18 screenplays.

Rich was actually a nom de plume for one Dalton Trumbo, a chain-smoking novelist and screenwriter with dark-rimmed glasses and an impeccably groomed moustache who, by this time, had already churned out such notable works as the anti-war novel *Johnny Got His Gun* and the screenplay for *Kitty Foil*. The former had been named the most original book of 1939 at the National Book Awards, and the latter had earned him an Oscar nomination five years later.

50 UNDEFEATED

He hadn't used the Robert Rich pen name back then, but pseudonyms had lately become a necessity. Trumbo had been held in contempt of Congress six years before the release of *The Brave One* for refusing to name names when called to testify before the House Un-American Activities Committee. This was the panel that had been formed during the McCarthy era to conduct investigations (translation: witch hunts) and expose alleged communist sympathizers.

Since then, he had been blacklisted, effectively cut off from getting any work as a screenwriter, because of his assumed identity as a communist sympathizer.

Trumbo, in fact, *had* been a member of the American Communist Party for five years. But by 1948, he had left the party. (He said he found the meetings "dull beyond description, and about as revolutionary in purpose as Wednesday evening testimonial services in the Christian Science Church.") Still, his involvement led to his subpoena as one of the so-called Hollywood Ten — a group of screenwriters, producers and directors called before the congressional committee.

Appearing before the panel, Trumbo refused to state whether he was a member of the Screen Writers Guild. It wasn't that he had anything to hide. It was a matter of principle.

"The rights of American labor to inviolably secret membership have been won in this country by a great cost of blood and a great cost in terms of hunger," he stated. "You asked me a question which would permit you to haul every union member in the United States up here to identify himself as a union member, to subject him to future intimidation and coercion. This, I believe, is an unconstitutional question."

The committee, however, either didn't agree or didn't care, and Trumbo was sentenced to prison for contempt. He served nearly a year behind bars in Kentucky before being released, and after that was placed on a blacklist that ensured he couldn't find work in his chosen profession — at least under his own name.

Instead, he began writing scripts under pseudonyms — one of them being "Robert Rich." It was under this name that he wrote *The Brave One*, the story of a young Mexican boy who rescues a calf born in the midst of a storm. He grows attached to the calf, which he keeps as a pet. But it soon grows into a strong and spirited bull, and the boy must fight to save him from death in the bullring.

Not only did the film win an Oscar for Best Writing, Motion Picture Story, but it also won a Golden Globe as Best Film Promoting International Understanding. The latter honor was somewhat ironic, as Trumbo received very little understanding from his accusers in Congress.

It wasn't the first time he had won an Academy Award incognito. Three years earlier, he had penned the story for a little film called *Roman Holiday*, with Audrey Hepburn and Gregory Peck. A friend, Ian McLellan Hunter, acted as a stand-in and claimed credit for the movie while turning the money over to Trumbo. Four decades after the film's 1953 release, Trumbo would receive the Academy Award posthumously.

At the time, he chafed against the injustice of it.

"This blacklisting is going to collapse, because it is rotten, immoral and illegal," he predicted. "I am one day going to be working openly in the motion picture industry."

And so he would.

As it turned out, Trumbo's biggest successes lay ahead. In 1959, Kirk Douglas hired him to write *Spartacus*, based on a novel by another blacklisted writer, Howard Fast. The story concerned a Thracian who had once been a Roman soldier but was later condemned to slavery and the life of a gladiator.

He and several other slaves succeeded in escaping and built a force of rebel slaves 70,000 strong to oppose the Romans in what became known as the Third Servile War (73-72 BCE). One of the film's most dramatic moments occurs when the Romans finally succeed in capturing Spartacus and his followers, then try to discover the identity of the rebel leader. As Spartacus, played by Douglas, is about to step forward, every member of the slave army responds by shouting, "I'm Spartacus!"

The slaves' refusal to disclose their leader's identity echoed the refusal of the Hollywood Ten to name names in their testimony before the House Un-American Activities Committee.

It may have been just one more example of a campaign Trumbo waged behind the scenes for some time to make a mockery of the blacklist. By this time, it was common knowledge that blacklisted writers had written screenplays for such classics as *Lawrence of Arabia* (Michael Wilson), Bridge on the River Kwai (Wilson) and *Inherit the Wind* (Nedrick Young).

Ring Lardner Jr., another blacklisted member of the Hollywood Ten, explained Trumbo's methods:

"A decisive factor in the ultimate collapse of the evil system was a campaign initiated and orchestrated by Dalton Trumbo that employed ridicule as a major means of demonstrating how unfair and contrary to American democratic principle the blacklist was. He saw to it that the media were made aware of every contradiction in the process."

When an award was presented to some writer using a pseudonym, Trumbo let that fact be known, Lardner said. When movies were attributed to Trumbo specifically, he coyly refused to confirm or deny his involvement. In doing so, he made the blacklisting process seem both unfair and untenable.

By the time the *Spartacus* project came along, the power of the blacklist was beginning to crumble altogether. At the beginning of 1959, the Academy of Motion Picture Arts and Sciences repealed a bylaw enforcing the blacklist; three days later, Trumbo identified himself as Robert Rich.

That same year, he was signed to work on *Spartacus*, this time using a different pseudonym — Sam Jackson. Trumbo's reputation as a fast writer (he reportedly could produce a 150-page script from start to finish in a single week) apparently impressed Kirk Douglas, who said Trumbo would go so far as writing while he was in the bathtub ... with a parrot on his shoulder.

Such unconventional methods seem to have worked.

"He was unbelievably talented," Douglas said. "And boy, he was fast. If he wrote something that didn't work, he'd throw it away and write something even better."

About the same time, Otto Preminger enlisted Trumbo to write the screenplay for another film, *Exodus*, based on a Leon Uris novel about the founding of Israel as a modern state. Preminger made no secret of the fact that he was hiring Trumbo for the project and that this time, the writer would not be hiding behind a pseudonym.

Both films came out in 1960, and both bore Trumbo's name, the Sam Jackson alter ego having been abandoned. The producers of *Spartacus*, seeking to gauge public reaction, had hired a market research firm to determine whether the Trumbo name was box office poison. But as it turned out, only 1 in 8 people who had heard of Trumbo said they would avoid the film if his name were in the credits. On the other hand, three times as many said they would be *more* likely to see the film if he were involved. Half of those who responded said it would make no difference.

Despite this favorable response, the American Legion protested the film on the basis of Trumbo's involvement. But President Kennedy helped ease the controversy by going to see the film, paving the way for the end of the blacklist as an effective tool for censorship.

He wasn't the only one who bought a ticket. In fact, the trade publication *Variety* reported in late December of 1960 that *Spartacus* and *Exodus* ranked No. 1 and No. 2 at the box office. Clearly, the viewers didn't mind Trumbo's name in the credits one bit — and were willing to say so with their wallets.

"The blacklist was a time of evil," he said, looking back, "and no one on either side who survived it came through untouched by evil."

Trumbo went on to write several more screenplays and enjoyed success over the next decade and a half. The Academy officially recognized him as the winner of the 1956 award for *The Brave One* in 1975, a year before he died.

"The only kind of love worth having is the kind that goes on living and laughing and fighting and loving."

— Dalton Trumbo

James Tillman
It's in the DNA

James Tillman's life wasn't what anyone would describe as perfect in the winter of 1988. He and two brothers had been brought up by a single mom who struggled to make ends meet working a minimum-wage job. Still, the 26-year-old African-American had a love of cars, and he was pursuing that interest when he landed a job at a car wash in Hartford, Conn.

In January of that year, an insurance company employee had just left a bar in downtown Hartford after having some drinks with coworkers. She was getting into her car when, out of nowhere, someone assaulted her. The man abducted her and drove her a few blocks to a church parking lot on Charter Oak Avenue, where he raped and beat her.

There were no witnesses to the brutal crime, so police took the woman down to the station and showed her a series of photographs, asking whether she could identify any of the men as her attacker.

She pointed to a picture of Tillman.

It wasn't long before authorities took him into custody and offered him a plea bargain that would have resulted in an eight-year sentence, but he protested his innocence and refused. He'd had minor brushes with the law before (which accounted for the presence of his photograph in the police file) but nothing like this, and he was not about to simply forfeit his freedom and his good name based on a false accusation.

So he stood up for what he believed in.

Himself.

For his trouble, he was convicted by an all-white jury and sentenced to 45 years in prison.

Jurors relied in part on incomplete DNA evidence in rendering their verdict, but based their decision primarily on the victim's testimony — and therein lay the difficulty. Eyewitness accounts are often unreliable, especially when they describe an event that took place at night or in the midst of a violent confrontation. And they can be even less trustworthy when they involve individuals of different races. The racist cliché that "they all look alike" conceals an even uglier reality: It's not a cliché. It's how people often view individuals of other races: not as individuals at all, but in terms broad-brush stereotypes.

The statistics confirm this.

Tillman, it seems, is hardly alone. More than half of the people who were wrongfully convicted and later cleared by DNA evidence had been initially identified — erroneously — by someone of a different race.

As a result, a disproportionate number of racial minorities wind up wrongly convicted. In all, 6 in 10 men who have been exonerated by an organization called the Innocence Project are African-Americans who have been wrongly convicted of raping white women — the same injustice that put Tillman behind bars.

The Innocence Project would play a crucial role for Tillman, as well, but not until he had spent more than a decade behind bars. At first, he has said, he was angry, but that anger took a backseat to the need to remain continually alert in his new surroundings. This was a treacherous place.

"You had to be on guard constantly," Tillman said. "These are dangerous people. Unpredictable."

Sometimes, it was hard to read people. When a fellow inmate said he'd been watching Tillman, it was easy enough to take it the wrong way — especially when the man was big and had a reputation for violence. But Tillman, it turned out, didn't need to be apprehensive on this occasion. The man was paying him a compliment. He actually viewed Tillman as a role model.

While Tillman was in prison, one of his brothers died of a heart condition, and the other wasn't allowed to visit him for the final eight years of his sentence because of a felony conviction of his own. His mother, however, came to visit every week, and the two would sing gospel songs to each other through the window that separated inmates from outsiders.

Tillman soon turned to the Bible for inspiration and began to adopt a more positive outlook. As part of this process, he pushed past the resentment he had toward the system that had put him behind bars, reasoning, "I can't serve the lord if I'm hating someone."

But Tillman wasn't destined to serve his full 45-year sentence. In 2005, some 16 years after his conviction, attorneys Karen Goodrow and Brian Carlow of the Innocence Project began looking into his case. They decided to examine the DNA evidence that had helped convict Tillman, using more advanced methods of analysis — methods that had become available since his incarceration.

What they found was significant. The new analysis excluded Tillman as a possible source for any of the DNA found on the rape victim's clothing. It all came from one person, and that person wasn't Tillman.

On June 6, 2006, the Superior Court of Connecticut vacated Tillman's conviction and granted his petition for a new trial. He was set free without bail, and a little more than a month later, all charges against him were dropped. He was the first prisoner to be freed as a result of work buy the Innocence Project.

Interestingly, the same DNA evidence that led to Tillman's acquittal led police to arrest a different man in the case. The new suspect, a man named Duane Foster, was being held in a Virginia jail in connection with burglary and larceny charges that had been filed in that state. He had once lived in Tillman's neighborhood and had actually served time with Tillman behind bars.

Foster couldn't be charged with rape because the statute of limitations for that crime had passed, but he could be charged with abducting someone for the purpose of committing a felony. In April of 2010, a judge asked him whether he was the person who had kidnapped the victim.

"Yes, I am," Foster answered.

And that's how Tillman's nightmare ended … or how it might have ended in a fairytale. But in the real world, though he found himself a free man, he was faced with the task of rebuilding a life that had been taken from him some 18 years earlier.

The governor proposed giving Tillman $500,000 as compensation for his time behind bars, but legislators thought that wasn't enough. In 2007, they passed a bill awarding him 10 times that amount — $5 million. The vote was 148-0 in the state House and 33-0 in the Senate.

"I think we all wonder, could we be so kind and gentle and humble as we find this person?" asked Rep. Kenneth Green. "He did not deserve to be incarcerated for 18½ years. Five million dollars is the least that we can do."

Since his release, Tillman has used his experience to motivate and counsel others. Less than two months after getting out of prison, he could be found speaking to teenage boys in Newington, Conn., as part of a mentoring program. When he noticed one boy falling asleep during his address, he saw a little of himself in the teen.

"I was the same way when I was your age," Tillman said. "Look at me. I went to prison for something I didn't do. What do you think will happen if you go out and actually do something that can land you in jail?"

Tillman married and eventually enrolled in Goodwin College, a private, nonprofit four-year institution in East Hartford, where he began pursuing a degree in human services.

His case also helped spark an interest in rooting out other cases of wrongful conviction in Connecticut and across the country. In 2010, Connecticut received a $1.5 million grant to review cases for any DNA evidence that might affect inmates convicted of crimes. In October 2012, a Louisiana man named Damon Thibodeaux released from death row became the 300th prisoner nationwide exonerated as a result of DNA evidence.

"I was innocent all along, so I just kept my faith and let science be science."

— James Tillman

Phillip Martin
Rebuilding a Nation

The biblical story of the Babylonian captivity is well known to anyone who took Sunday School classes in childhood. According to that account, King Nebuchadnezzar ordered that the population of Jerusalem and the surrounding area be forcibly deported to the heart of his empire, where they and their families stayed for more than half a century.

That was 2,600 years ago.

What's less well known is that a similar forced deportation occurred less than two centuries ago, when the majority of the Choctaw Nation was uprooted from its homeland in Alabama, Louisiana and Mississippi and exiled to Oklahoma. Under the Treaty of Dancing Rabbit, the Choctaw gave up some 11 million acres of land to the U.S. government and were evicted from their ancestral land.

During their forced march westward, hundreds perished from disease, hunger and exposure to the elements.

They called it the "Trail of Tears."

By 1930, fewer than two thousand Choctaw remained on their land. Phillip Martin's family was one of those that stayed in Mississippi, but conditions were no better for those left behind than they were for the departed. Born the third of six children in a time and place known for its bigotry toward people of native ancestry, Martin's family scraped by on the wages his father earned as a janitor.

Later, when his father was killed by a hit-and-run driver, they were forced to rely on welfare.

Martin's mother eventually sent him away to a Cherokee boarding school in North Carolina, and he joined the Army at age 19, becoming a radar technician. He later joined the Air Force, where he served for ten years and rose to the rank of staff sergeant before returning to Mississippi upon being discharged and using the G.I. Bill as a means to become an electrician.

Martin soon became involved in tribal leadership and was eventually elected chief in 1979. At the time, the Mississippi Choctaw community was so desolate and impoverished that three-quarters of its members were unemployed. Many lived in shanties along dirt roads, some apparently unable to even fully clothe their young children. Those who did work were manual laborers or agricultural workers.

Under Martin's leadership, things got better. The year he assumed leadership, the Choctaw completed an 80-acre industrial park. From there, he spearheaded the development of more than a dozen businesses owned by the Choctaw people. They became one of the biggest employers in the state, creating more than nine thousand jobs — including seven thousand at the Pearl River Resort, a complex that includes two hotel casinos, a water park and golf course.

Other companies included a direct mail business, a printer, a construction company and a plastics molding facility.

"He was truly one of the first and most important leaders in the drive for tribal self-determination," said Joseph Kalt of the Harvard Project on American Indian Economic Development. "Chief Martin led this movement in which first the Mississippi Choctaw and then many other Indian nations said, 'We're going to run everything ourselves. We're building our own schools, our own police department, our own health program, our own economy."

By the time Martin left office in 2007, after nearly three decades leading the Mississippi Choctaw, the tribal nation's unemployment rate was just 4 percent. Life expectancy among the tribe had risen by two full decades, the shanties of earlier years had been replaced by suburban homes.

"We decided if we were going to live here, we should try to do something for ourselves," Martin said in 1986. "Our success has changed the attitudes not only of the Choctaw but of our neighbors."

When Martin died in 2010, the Wall Street Journal headlined his obituary as follows:

"Moses of the Choctaws Led the Indian Tribe to Prosperity."

"If you don't improve your community, you're going to lose it. You will lose your language, your culture."

— Phillip Martin

STEPHEN H. PROVOST

John Scopes
Misdirection Play

This high school football coach had an interesting strategy when he was accused of a crime he didn't commit.

He confessed to it and fought it in court.

He lost.

But the battle is still being fought today, nearly a century after this classic misdirection play sent the state of Tennessee — and the nation — into an uproar. It involved a three-time loser in presidential politics, an opportunistic businessman and the aforementioned football coach, who also happened to be a classroom teacher.

He came to prominence during the age of Knute Rockne and Red Grange, when the sport was beginning to gain in popularity. But you won't find this particular coach's name in any athletic hall of fame, because he's not famous for football. Just 24 years old at the time, he's known today for a court case that was set in motion by a meeting with businessman George Rappalyea at a drugstore in Dayton, Tenn.

The three-time presidential also-ran, a master orator named William Jennings Bryan, had been on a crusade to ban textbooks that taught Charles Darwin's theory of evolution and had lobbied more than a dozen states to introduce legislation to this effect. One of these was Tennessee, which had recently passed a bill called the Butler Act that made it illegal to "teach any theory that denies the story of divine creation as taught in the Bible and to teach instead that man was descended from lower animals."

The American Civil Liberties Union had stated that it would pay to challenge the Butler Act in court if it could find a teacher willing to act as the defendant. That's where businessman Rappalyea, a geologist who owned a coal company, came into the picture. He approached the football coach/teacher with the idea of serving as the defendant in such a case.

The coach, John T. Scopes, consented.

Rappalyea wanted H.G. Wells to defend Scopes, but the science fiction author wasn't interested, so Clarence Darrow took the job. Bryan himself led the prosecution, even though he hadn't practiced law in three decades, and thousands arrived to watch the trial. Defenders of the Bible waved copies of evangelist T.T. Martin's book *Hell and the High Schools*, wherein the author lamented the "scourge" of "scholastic paganism" that he warned was "sweeping our young men and women, boys and girls, away from God ... and into hell for eternity."

Not only were those who credited evolution supposedly going to hell, Bryan complained the concept was positively un-American. After all, he said, it contended that humans descended "not even from American monkeys, but Old World monkeys."

Darrow, whose planned use of expert witnesses had been derailed when the judge disallowed them, responded by calling Bryan himself to the stand and getting him to admit that the six days of creation described in Genesis might not have been meant literally.

Though he was embarrassed on the stand, Bryan still won the case, and Scopes was fined $100, but it was a hollow victory in many respects. Even Bryan himself didn't get much chance to enjoy it. He died in his sleep six days later.

An appellate court overturned the case on a technicality, noting that the jury should have set the fine rather than the judge, but the state's high court refused to act further, declaring that nothing was to be gained by "prolonging the life of this bizarre case." As a result the

Butler Act stayed on the books for more than four decades after the trial's conclusion, finally being repealed in 1967.

Scopes died only three years after that, having returned to school shortly after the trial for graduate studies in geology at the University of Chicago. He eventually went to work as a geologist for the United Gas Company and was baptized into the Roman Catholic Church in 1930. It turned out to be a prescient choice. Twenty years later, Pope Pius XII declared that the church would not forbid that "research and discussions ... take place with regard to the doctrine of evolution."

Other religious leaders, however, have been slower to endorse the theory Darwin put forth more than a century and a half ago, though it has long been universally accepted by scientists. Other presidential candidates have even followed in Bryan's footsteps by touting creationism or intelligent design as viable Bible-based alternatives to evolution.

Perhaps the supreme irony of it all is that Scopes wasn't even guilty of teaching evolution. According to a story filed by William Kinsey Hutchinson for William Randolph Hearst's International News Service, Scopes confided to him during the waning days of the trial: "I didn't violate the law. ... I never taught that evolution session. I skipped it. I was doing something else the day I should have taught it, and I missed the whole lesson about Darwin and never did teach it."

Hutchinson agreed not to publish Scopes' confession until after the case's last appeal had been decided.

No doubt William Jennings Bryan was rolling over in his grave. But Knute Rockne would have been proud.

"What goes on in the classroom is up to the student and the teacher. Once you introduce the power of the state ... you've become involved in propaganda."

— John Scopes

Joseph Shabalala
Chopping Down Apartheid

It might be tempting to say that Joseph Shabalala became famous because he and his band appeared on an album by Paul Simon. Tempting, but not entirely accurate.

While Simon's CD *Graceland* brought Shabalala to the attention of new American audiences, the prolific musician and founder of the South African choral group Ladysmith Black Mambazo had already made more than twice as many records as Simon had — including his collaborations with Art Garfunkel — by the time that album was released in 1986.

The group was the result of a dream Shabalala had when he was in his early twenties.

"I had a dream of a type of singing group that I wanted to create," Shabalala remembered. "Not just a dream, in a wishful way, but an actual dream while I was asleep. This beautiful dream led to the creation of my group, Ladysmith Black Mambazo."

He heard the sound of children singing and began looking for them. There was a stage, but the children weren't on the stage — they were floating between the stage and the sky, teaching him the style of singing he sought to emulate.

"I start to copy those harmonies," he said, "because from our fathers at the time, the sound was not exactly correct. I was always thinking about how can I describe this music until I started to have that sound from the dream."

Shabalala named the group for his hometown of Ladysmith, the black ox and an ax (*mambazo* in the Zulu tongue) that was chosen as a reference to the way the group would routinely "chop down" its rivals in the competitions they entered.

But for a black choir performing in South Africa during the apartheid era, it was no simple matter to chop down the racist obstacles that often confronted the group. When the band started performing, it was illegal for blacks to travel around the country without "permission"). The choir, however, had an ace in the hole: their music.

Whenever they were pulled over, they would simply start to sing. Shabalala's cousin and fellow choir member Albert Mazibuko said the trick worked every time, and the police simply let them go.

Well, not quite every time.

On one occasion, a police commissioner hauled them into court, informing them they needed permission like everyone else. But when they appeared before the magistrate, they opened their mouths again ... and out came this enthralling music. The magistrate, Shabalala said, "was so taken aback, and he took his glasses off and said, 'Wow, this is beautiful.'"

Needless to say, the group received the necessary permission.

The band performed its songs a cappella in a Zulu style known as isicathamiya, a word that stems from a root that means "to walk softly" or "tread lightly." Such discretion was necessary in the era of apartheid, a post-World War II policy implemented by the white ruling class to repress and isolate indigenous peoples.

Ironically, apartheid was being codified about the same time U.S. segregation policies in the South were coming under increasing attack by the nascent civil rights movement. It was the work of the Afrikaner government, dominated by the descendants of Dutch (and some English) colonists.

Under this policy, South Africans were classified into four racial groups: native (black), white, colored (mixed race) and Asian. Some jobs were to be filled only by white workers, and intermarriage between whites and members of the other groups was strictly prohibited.

It wasn't long before the segregation went further. In 1951, several reservations were created, and Africans were restricted to these areas. The government sought to justify its actions by maintaining that the lands in question were the original "homelands" of the groups in question. But in fact, many of those who were uprooted had no connection at all to the lands where they were sent, and those lands constituted just 13 percent of South African territory. The white ruling class got the rest.

As with any exercise in segregation, the results were separate ... and anything but equal. "I have seen very few countries in the world that have such inadequate educational conditions," World Bank President Robert McNamara said on a visit to South Africa in 1982. "I was shocked at what I saw in some of the rural areas and homelands."

This wasn't a matter of granting autonomy. It was, instead, a concerted attempt by the government of South Africa to wash its hands of any responsibility for the vast majority of those within its borders. What the homeland policy amounted to was an exercise in internal deportation. Blacks were relocated and eventually found themselves deprived of South African citizenship; in fact, they needed a passport to leave their assigned territories.

This was problematic because most of the so-called homelands were surrounded by South African territory — with some being split into two or more pieces. Hence, the internal exiles wound up virtual prisoners on islands of territory that were far too small to be truly self-sufficient and almost entirely dependent upon South Africa for their wellbeing.

Large populations — 81 percent of the people — were packed onto small parcels of land that lacked the resources to support them, and residents were exploited as poorly paid manual laborers in the nation's gold, mineral, asbestos and coal mines. It was in the mines that the workers developed the style of isicathamiya, singing to keep their spirits up. The music was an important distraction and source of comfort amid the often inhuman conditions under which they toiled. Apartheid researcher Alan B. Durning remarked that "for every ton of gold South Africa extracts, a black miner dies in an accident that would have been unlikely in other countries."

Apartheid led to the exploitation of both the black population and the environment. In describing the homelands, Durning drew a picture of territories poor in natural resources and ill-suited to the development of a self-sustaining economy: "By design, these areas are remote, their topsoil is thin, rainfall is scarce and unreliable, and the ground sloping and rocky."

In 1978, there was one doctor for every 400 white people, but one for every 44,000 blacks. The government spent nearly $700 a year on white students. For black students, the figure was $45. Infant mortality among blacks was 10 to 20 times what it was for whites.

Shabalala (full name Bhekizizwe Joseph Siphatimandla Mxoveni Mshengu Bigboy Shabalala) was born in 1941 in an area that would become one of the homelands: KwaZulu-Natal. But a nation where a repressive minority sought to isolate itself (and its wealth) from the vast majority of its people had a powerful force working against it. A unifying force: Music.

"The music was the key," Shabalala said. "It was like something that bridged the gap. The music played a big role to bring these two nations together, because music knows no boundaries. White people supported us secretly in those days, but they were not allowed to say anything. Our people, they get strength through the music."

In fact, the music of Ladysmith Black Mambazo was so appealing across racial lines that they were able to land a recording contract — a privilege that was normally reserved for whites. Not only did they win over police officers who would have normally demanded their papers, they gained white fans, as well.

"I remember a white family — they never missed a show, said Mazibuko, Shabalala's cousin, who joined the group in 1970. "One evening during the performance, the police came and took them away. It was a black people's area, so they were not allowed to be there. Those things were affecting us so deeply. We sing songs of peace and unity and encourage people to unite for our freedom."

That message of unity, however, was not without controversy. Some black fans accused them of selling out because they — unlike other black groups — were allowed to record their music and sell records. Then, when they took part in the *Graceland* project, they faced criticism from the other side because Simon had broken an anti-apartheid cultural embargo to record with them.

Regardless of one's position on Simon's actions, there is little argument that the resulting CD did what Shabalala had intended to do. Once again, he was using music to bridge the cultural gap.

Shabalala co-wrote two tracks with Simon — *Homeless* and *Diamonds on the Soles of Her Shoes* — for the album, which won a Grammy for Album of the Year. It is still acknowledged as perhaps the pinnacle of Simon's solo career... even though it's anything but a solo album. In addition to Ladysmith Black Mambazo, it employs the talents of numerous other African musicians, as well as the likes of Linda Ronstadt, Los Lobos, and the Everly Brothers.

The release went to No. 1 on the charts and wound up selling nearly 16 million copies — just shy of the figure posted by Simon and Garfunkel's iconic *Bridge Over Troubled Waters*. It ranks fifth among *Rolling Stone*'s top 100 for the decade in which it was released stood at No. 71 on the magazine's all-time list as of 2012.

"It will stay with us forever," Mazibuko said. "That took us to the next level of music."

A year later, the group had won a Grammy of its own for Best World Music Recording on its Simon-produced album *Shaka Zulu*.

"Scholars came to the airport to welcome us," Shabalala recalled more than a decade later. "It was the first time that a South African had won a Grammy Award... That's why we had the power to create the South African Traditional Music Association. Once you've won something, you have power."

A few years later, apartheid was abolished, and Shabalala's group sang at the inauguration of the nation's first black president, Nelson Mandela in 1994. Ladysmith Black Mambazo also accompanied Mandela to the Nobel Peace Prize ceremony in Oslo, and the group later performed for Queen Elizabeth at Buckingham Palace.

Even with these high points, Shabalala's quest for peace and unity was at times interrupted by tragedy. In 1991, his brother Headman Shabalala was killed in an apparent racial murder committed by an off-duty white security guard. Eleven years later, Nellie, his wife of 30 years, was fatally shot outside their home, and his daughter became ill and died. Then, in 2004, another brother died a violent death when he was shot while driving his children to school.

Still, Shabalala remained dedicated to a message rooted in his Christian philosophy and to his music.

"Singing is just like kneeling down and praying," he said. "I remember the first day when I listened to harmony. It calmed my heart. And from that day, up to today, music is just like my pillar. I lean against that harmony."

"I must carry on singing. That is my prayer. That is my comfort. There is nothing else."

— Joseph Shabalala

Babe Didrikson Zaharias
World's Greatest Athlete

With a name like Mildred and a hobby like sewing, one might be surprised to find that the winner of the South Texas State Fair blue ribbon in 1931 was criticized for being ... not feminine enough. She had excelled at tap-dancing and was even married to a man in the one of the most masculine lines of work you could imagine.

Still, one magazine writer groused that "it would be much better if she and her ilk stayed at home, got themselves prettied up and waited for the phone to ring."

She wouldn't have had to wait very long.

The best way to overcome such chauvinistic talk was to outrun it (on the track). Or shoot it down (on the basketball court), or drive her point home (on the golf course). Truth be told, she did all these things better than she could sew, and she did them better than the guys could, too.

Mildred "Babe" Didrikson Zaharias was a one-woman, multi-sport athletic wrecking crew. And no, that's not an exaggeration, as she demonstrated convincingly at the 1932 amateur track and field championships in Evanston, Ill. She entered the event as the only member of the Employers Casualty Insurance Company team from Dallas.

The team that finished second at the event had 22 members.

The team that finished first was ...the Employers Casualty Insurance Company team from Dallas.

Yep. Didrikson (she wasn't yet married at the time) won the event all by her lonesome. Running from one event to the next, she placed first in one after the other, setting a total of four world records in the process:

The long jump.
The shot put (world record).
The javelin (world record).
The hurdles (world record).
The baseball throw (world record).

Oh, yeah. And she tied for first in another event, the high jump, an event in which she won a silver medal at the Los Angeles Olympics that same summer. It was one of three medals she won at those Games (the others coming in the javelin and hurdles), and the only one that wasn't gold.

"The Babe is here," she used to say. "Who's coming in second?"

Didrikson's time in the 80-meter hurdles at the Games was another world record at 11.7 seconds. She would have won the high jump, too, under modern rules. The only reason she finished second was a judge's ruling that her head had cleared the bar before the rest of her body went over — a distinction that's no longer part of the rules.

"She bragged, she swore, drank, but could be presented at court ... or sew a dress for herself as well as the product of any finishing school," Los Angeles Times sportswriter Jim Murray once wrote. "She was a roughneck with a basketball or a deck of cards in her hands. But she grew roses, raised poodles, danced at the White House and hung curtains like the dutiful Scandinavian housewife she was."

Didrikson's performance at the Olympics came near the outset of what would be perhaps the most dominant and diverse athletic career of the 20th century. The Associated Press would select Zaharias as its female athlete of the year six times, but only once on the basis of her performance as a track athlete.

She was never named athlete of the year as a basketball player, even though she once scored 106 points in a game and achieved AAU All-American status in that sport from 1930-32.

She didn't win the award for her prowess as a bowler, though she once rolled a 237 game and boasted an average of 170.

She never earned the accolade as a baseball player, even though she earned the nickname "Babe" after hitting five home runs in a baseball game during her childhood, and even though she pitched one inning for the Philadelphia Athletics in a preseason game against the Brooklyn Dodgers in 1934. She also played for the House of David, a semipro barnstorming team, at one point pitching to Joe DiMaggio. She struck him out on three pitches.

After another outing, St. Louis Cardinals pitcher Burleigh Grimes (a future Hall of Famer) remarked that "Babe Didrikson would be one of the best prospects in baseball if she were a boy."

And therein lay the rub.

During the 1930s, Didrikson's legend grew through a series of highly publicized appearances — some of which were taken to ludicrous extremes. She appeared in one film that showed her participating in 12 different sporting events, including a partially staged appearance on the football field with the Southern Methodist squad. In another instance, she appeared at a photo shoot that made it appear as though she had knocked out a professional boxer. Another proposed stunt would have had her run against a horse; she almost agreed before passing on the opportunity.

But lest anyone doubt that she was still an athlete to be reckoned with (no stunts required), Didrikson erased it by taking on yet another athletic challenge: the golf course. It was in this sport that she would earn her five other female athlete of the year awards.

Ironically, she once remarked, "Most things come natural to me, and golf was the first that ever gave me much trouble."

Didrikson, however, had made up her mind she was going to master the game, laying down the gantlet for herself in 1933 by proclaiming, "I have enough money to last me three years, and I intend to win the women's amateur golf championship before these three years — and my bankroll — are gone."

She practiced from 9 a.m. until midnight.

She practiced until her hands bled and her coach had to force her to wear gloves.

But she didn't win the amateur title. After rallying to capture the Texas State Tournament in 1935, Didrikson was ruled ineligible to compete for the amateur title because she had earned a significant sum of money on an exhibition tour with career Grand Slam winner Gene Sarazen. On the plus side, the tour had enabled her to avoid running through her entire bankroll in three years, as she had forecast.

So she had a little more time.

Didrikson entered the Los Angeles Open — a men's tournament — in 1938, becoming the first woman to try such a feat. She missed the cut but met her future husband, George Zaharias, with whom she was teamed. She eventually gained back her amateur status, and in 1946 won that U.S. Women's Amateur title she had set out to claim back in 1933.

A year later, she took things one step further and became the first woman to ever win the British Ladies Amateur tournament. Meanwhile, she continued to enter men's tournaments, as well. And unlike her previous appearance at the Los Angeles Open, where she failed to qualify for the final two rounds, this time she made the cut.

Didrikson became the first woman in history to do so when she returned to the L.A. Open in 1945, then duplicated the feat by making the cut at the Phoenix Open and Tucson Open. Returning to women's competition, she won 17 consecutive amateur events before turning pro. She sought to play in the U.S. Open men's tournament but was barred from qualifying when the organizers declared that "applicants must be men who are either professional golfers or amateurs with handicaps not exceeding three strokes. Thus, the U.S.G.A. has declined an informal entry submitted on behalf of Mrs. George Zaharias."

Zaharias' rejoinder: "I only wanted to qualify. I still think I'm good enough to play."

Indeed, she was so good that she joined 12 other women in forming the LPGA, where she not only competed but also served as president from 1952-55. The tour was created in part to showcase her skills, and she did not fail to disappoint, promptly dominating it through its first four years.

Didrikson won a total of 31 events on the tour and was the top money-winner four years running. She reached 10 wins faster than any other golfer, setting a record that still stood in 2012, but was slowed by a colon cancer diagnosis in 1953. She underwent surgery and won the U.S. Women's Open one month later while wearing a colostomy bag.

Her margin of victory: a whopping 12 strokes.

"I expect to play golf until I am 90," she said, "even longer if anybody figures out a way to swing a club from a rocking chair."

Sadly, however, she never got that chance. The cancer returned in 1955 and, although she continued competing that year (winning two of the eight events she entered), Didrikson died in September of the following year.

She was just 45 years old.

As of 2012, she still ranked among the top 10 all-time winners on the LPGA Tour, even though she competed at a time when far fewer tournaments were held. And she holds one world record in track and field that will never be broken. Her 1931 world-record baseball throw of 296 feet stood for 26 years before the event was discontinued.

No wonder Joe DiMaggio struck out.

"She is beyond all belief until you see her perform," sportswriter Grantland Rice once said. "Then you finally understand that you are looking at the most flawless section of muscle harmony, of complete mental and physical coordination, the world of sport has ever seen."

50 UNDEFEATED

"All my life I have always had the urge to do things better than anybody else."

— Babe Didrikson Zaharias

STEPHEN H. PROVOST

Malala Yousafzai
Daughter of Pakistan

Bullying at school is never harmless. Kids often call classmates names, taunt them and sometimes hit them. They might threaten them if they don't hand over their lunch money … or that new pair of Air Jordans. Any of these things can be bad enough.

Now imagine that the bullies aren't kids, but adults. You're the target of those bullies. And imagine that, instead of beating you up, they shoot you. In the head. On the school bus.

That's what happened to Malala Yousafzai, a 14-year-old student in Pakistan who dared to obtain an education and encourage other girls to do so. In many parts of the world, this would have been no big deal. Laudable, yes. But dangerous? Hardly.

In Yousafzai's home, the Swat Valley of Pakistan, the situation was radically different. As of this writing, the district's official website still describes it as "a paradise on earth." Some people called it "the Switzerland of Pakistan."

So it was until recently. Tall mountains stood watch over a verdant valley floor that was home to forestland, roaring rivers and ancient Buddhist ruins. Pakistani vacationers joined foreign tourists in flocking to the area for its trout fishing, skiing (it was home to the only ski resort in the country) and sheer beauty.

The war in neighboring Afghanistan, however, helped change all that. The area was home to many ethic Afghans, and militants from the ousted Taliban regime began to cross the border from Afghanistan into Pakistan. Meanwhile, an Islamic militant named Maulana Fazlullah began broadcasting a call to holy war from several illegal radio stations in the Swat district.

Militants responded.

By 2008, some 4,000 rebels had begun an uprising that plunged the Swat Valley into chaos. Few dared to visit the region's resorts, and the once-tranquil and alluring landscape became scarred by violence, the air filled with the sounds of explosions and the tortured cries of its victims. Nearly half of the region's 1.8 million residents fled. The rest became subject to a way of life that would have once been unthinkable.

It was in the midst of these horrors that Yousafzai began chronicling events as they unfolded in a blog reproduced by the BBC. She chose the pen name Gul Makai, which means "sunflower" and belonged to the heroine of a Pakistani folktale. In the story, as in *Romeo and Juliet*, a romance between Gul Makai and her lover leads to a war between their two rival tribes. Unlike Shakespeare's classic, however, there's a happy ending: Gul Makai uses the Qur'an to illustrate that the grounds for the war are frivolous and persuades religious leaders to intervene in the conflict — which is ultimately resolved when the two lovers are united in marriage.

The name, Yousafzai explained, was far preferable to her given name, which means "grief-stricken."

It reflected her hope, even amid the direst circumstances.

The continual threat of violence, she wrote, gave her nightmares: "I had a terrible dream yesterday with military helicopters and the Taleban," she wrote in an entry titled *I Am Afraid* dated Jan. 3, 2009. "I have had such dreams since the launch of the military operation in Swat. ...

"On my way from school to home I heard a man saying 'I will kill you.' I hastened my pace and after a while looked back (to see) if the man was still coming behind me. But to my utter relief he was talking on his mobile and must have been threatening someone else over the phone."

At the end of the year, Fazlullah banned all girls from receiving an education, and some 2,000 schools for girls were bombed or set ablaze.

"My friend came to me and said, 'For God's sake, answer me honestly, is our school going to be attacked by the Taleban?'" Yousafzai wrote Jan 5. "During the morning, we were told not to wear colourful clothes as the Taleban might object to it."

She feared her school wouldn't reopen after the winter break because of Fazlullah's decree. The principal, she said, had announced the start of the break but had neglected to give a date for the girls' return to class. He had always done so in the past, and his failure to follow the same practice now led Yousafzai to an inescapable conclusion. "The principle did not inform us about the reason behind not announcing the school reopening," she wrote, "but my guess was that the Taleban had announced a ban on girls' education from 15 January."

As Yousafzai had predicted, many schools declined to reopen after the break, leaving some 80,000 girls without any classes to attend. Meanwhile, the violence was only getting worse. The day after school let out, Yousafzai wrote that "the night was filled with the noise of artillery fire and I woke up three times."

The following month, the Pakistani government brokered a peace agreement with Fazlullah's father-in-law, Taliban leader Maulana Sufi Muhammad. Under the terms of the deal, Pakistan's government agreed to a Taliban demand that the area be governed under a strict interpretation of Islamic law. In exchange, the Taliban pledged to end the violence.

Instead of peace, however, the deal only served as an excuse for the Taliban to consolidate — and seek to expand — their power. None of the destroyed girls' schools was rebuilt. Women were ordered to stay at home, and men were told they must grow beards and don prayer caps.

Those accused of transgressing the law could look forward to being flogged publicly or even beheaded.

Or they could be attacked.

That's what happened to Yousafzai on Oct. 9, 2012, when she and her fellow students were on their way home from school. It had been four years since the Taliban takeover of Swat, and the Pakistani government had managed to retake control of the area after the Taliban failed to honor their end of the peace deal.

Yousafzai's family had been displaced in the government offensive, but with the expulsion of the Taliban forces, they were allowed to return to their hometown of Mingora, the largest city in Swat. During their exile and afterward, Yousafzai continued her activism. She took part in a documentary and gave interviews to several media outlets. In addition, she led the District Child Assembly of Swat and earned a nomination (courtesy of Desmond Tutu) for the International Children's Peace Prize in October 2011. Two months later, she was named the first winner of the National Youth Peace Prize for Pakistan.

All of this made her a target.

The school bus on which she was riding rumbling along toward Mingora about 12:30 in the afternoon when two men riding bicycles flagged it down just outside of town. The pair got on board, and one of them immediately started waving a gun.

"Which one of you is Malala Yousafzai?" he asked. "Speak up! Otherwise, I will shoot you all."

No one said a word.

"She is propagating against the soldiers of Allah, the Taliban. She must be punished!"

Then, somehow, the gunman recognized Yousafzai. Pointing the gun at the teenager, he fired, wounding her in the head and neck — the bullet reportedly grazed her brain. Two other shots injured two other passengers before the assailant and his accomplice fled.

Shazia Ramzan, a friend of Malala's who sat next to her and was also shot, recalled the sudden horror of the scene: "It was just a normal school day," she said. "We were coming home after our second-term exams. The bus was taking its usual route. Then suddenly it stopped and two men confronted us."

When one of them started shooting, she said, "Malala fell to the floor unconscious. There was blood everywhere. I was in total shock. Then the man with the gun fired at me and another girl and ran away. We were just so traumatized and shocked. Everything happened so quickly."

Amazingly, Yousafzai was not paralyzed in the attack, but she remained in a medically induced coma for about a week as doctors worked frantically to keep her alive and get her out of danger.

The Taliban issued several statements claiming responsibility for the shooting. "We are dead against co-education and a secular education system," one of them said. Added another: "We warned her several times to stop speaking against the Taliban. This is a clear message for the rest of the youth as well. Whoever is found following Yousafzai will meet the same fate."

Much of Pakistan, however, didn't seem to care. President Asif Ali Zardari called Yousafzai "a symbol of all that is good about us. Malala represents the resilience of our girls and women. Her attackers aren't just trying to kill the Daughter of Pakistan. They are trying to kill Pakistan." Meanwhile, thousands marched to support Yousafzai as she lay unconscious in a hospital. It was far from clear whether she would survive.

Before long, the teenager's brain started to swell, and she was moved from Pakistan to a medical facility in Birmingham, England, where she received further treatment. Despite fears for her life, Yousafzai was eventually revived from her coma and, less than two weeks after the attack, she managed to stand for the first time.

Meanwhile, the investigation into the attempt on her life focused on none other than Fazlullah, whose ability to conduct paramilitary strikes had been curtailed by government forces after the failed peace agreement of 2009. His ability to use terror as a weapon to strike fear into those who dared oppose Taliban edicts, however, was undiminished. A group of about 100 terrorists who specialized in targeted killing remained under his command.

A spokesman for the Fazlullah's group described how, "before the attack, the two fighters personally collected information about Malala's route to school, timing, the vehicle she used and her security." The decision was made to attack her near a military checkpoint, he said, to emphasize that the group was capable of striking with impunity.

"We have a clear-cut stance," he said. "Anyone who takes side with the government against us will have to die at our hands. You will see. Other important people will soon become victims."

The stance of those on the other side of the question, however, is just as clear-cut. Yousafzai's father Ziauddin, who has himself been threatened by the Taliban, vowed not to be intimidated by threats. Instead, he pledged to return to Pakistan once she his daughter had recovered and continue the fight for educational freedom.

When his daughter spoke to him, she voiced the same intent, expressing confidence in her recovery and an eagerness to resume her studies: "She told me ... 'Please bring me my books of Class 9, and I will attend my examination in Swat.'"

"The girls of Swat aren't afraid of anyone."

— Malala Yousafzai

STEPHEN H. PROVOST

Lou Ferrigno
Simply Incredible

Years before Mark Ruffalo, Eric Bana or Edward Norton turned green to play Bruce Banner and his alter ego, Lou Ferrigno was the most incredible Hulk of all. This was the 1970s, when the CGI technology that would create such fantastic illusions for the Marvel Cinematic Universe was still decades away. So, when CBS decided to do a TV version of Stan Lee's superhero comic book, it had to go old school.

Bill Bixby, who had starred in My Favorite Martian and The Courtship of Eddie's Father, had already been cast as Banner (whose name was changed to David for the show), but Bixby — at 5-foot-9 and 170 pounds — wasn't a physically imposing actor. In fact, the story was built around the fact that a slightly built, brilliant scientist could be transformed into a physically imposing, menacing monster who spoke mostly in grunts and growls.

Bixby could play Banner, but he couldn't play the Hulk; a different actor was needed for that assignment.

Arnold Schwarzenegger was considered for the role, but although he was no slouch at 6-foot-2, the producers thought he was too short to make it work. Besides, Schwarzenegger hadn't done much acting. A former powerlifting champion and a six-time Mr. Olympia as a bodybuilder, he was still four years away from his breakout film role in Conan the Barbarian.

So the studio turned to an actor who was tall. Really tall. Richard Kiel had played a giant caveman called Eegah, had appeared in The Longest Yard with Burt Reynolds and had portrayed the James Bond villain known as Jaws. The former nightclub bouncer's imposing physique was the result of a condition called acromegaly: an excess of human growth hormone. At 7 feet, 2 inches, he was certainly tall enough to play the Hulk, but he just wasn't buff enough. He couldn't even convince Kiel's son, who was on the set to watch the filming.

The boy protested that his father just didn't have what it took to play the Hulk. He lacked the big muscles and big shoulders, like the comic book.

That's where Lou Ferrigno came in.

Ferrigno, like Schwarzenegger, was a bodybuilder by trade who hadn't done much acting at that point. But at 6-foot-5, he was bigger than Schwarzenegger and more muscular than Kiel. In fact, he'd appeared with Schwarzenegger just one year earlier in the movie Pumping Iron, which documented Schwarzenegger's final Mr. Olympia title (Ferrigno, winner of back-to-back Mr. Universe crowns and the youngest person ever to claim that title, finished third).

Winning the role as the Hulk was a form of poetic justice. Ferrigno had been motivated to pursue bodybuilding by comic book heroes like the Hulk. When he was just a toddler, he'd suffered an ear infection that caused him to lose 80 percent of his hearing, which led to teasing and bullying in school.

"They used to call me 'deaf Louie,' 'deaf mute,' because of my hearing and the way I sounded" — even though he'd taught himself to read lips, his speech was less precise. He told Oprah Winfrey: "I was difficult to understand, I was very introverted. I was thin, I was small, and I was afraid to fight back."

His relationship with his father compounded the problem. Matty Ferrigno was a New York City police lieutenant who, like some of Lou's peers, had no patience for his hearing and speech problems, and would later castigate him for losing to Schwarzenegger.

His father favored his younger brother, and Lou said: "I wanted to prove (myself) so my father would love me." Unfortunately, however, "the relationship didn't improve at all." "I have a very, ah, abusive father," he said during an interview in the early '90s, when he came out of retirement as a bodybuilder and returned to competition. "I couldn't speak, so the thoughts where, I was told as a kid, 'You can't do it, you can't do it. You're never going to make anything. But I was very driven and ... I learned quickly, knowing that (if you) believe and trust in yourself, you can't go wrong. If you have other people influence you, you will become what they want you to become."

Determined not to feel sorry for himself, so he responded to his peers' bullying and his father's abuse by seeking to empower himself. Literally.

Inspired by superheroes, he took up bodybuilding at the age of 13, attaching cans of concrete to a broomstick because he couldn't afford his own dumbbells.

"That," he said, "was the path for me to survive" and to gain respect. "I would pull my hearing aid out and completely tune out the rest of the world, and fantasize that these superheroes were me."

Ferrigno's first larger-than-life role model was Superman, portrayed in a popular 1950s TV series by George Reeves. Ferrigno was a fan of the show, but as a young boy, he thought the red-caped Kryptonian was a real person. Seeking to emulate the Man of Steel, he grabbed a red blanket, climbed up to the second story of his apartment building, and jumped off.

Alas, he couldn't fly.

"When I hit the concrete, that was the end of reading the Superman comic," he said. From then on, he started focusing more on the Hulk.

Why the Hulk?

"The Hulk was a unique character because of his strength and power," Ferrigno explained. "He doesn't have a costume like Spider-

Man or Superman — the Hulk is more visual. His passion and his strength, that is what separates him from anything else."

Ferrigno didn't have to speak in his role as the Hulk, but he did go on to do more acting, after the show ended its five-season run, starring in the 1983 film Hercules and a sequel two years later. He later appeared in guest roles on TV shows including Night Court and Chuck, as well as 20 episodes of The King of Queens. In 2012, he received an implant that restored his hearing.

That same year, he was sworn in as a reserve deputy in California's San Luis Obispo County, and in 2020, he became a sheriff's deputy in New Mexico.

"Bodybuilding saved my life."

— Lou Ferrigno

Hanne Gaby Odiele
Role Model

Some people are different in ways that aren't readily apparent, but they know that if they reveal how they're different, acceptance could change to ridicule — or demands that they change. That something can be sexual orientation, nationality, religious creed. Or it might involve being intersex.

Intersex is the "I" in LGBTQIA, but it's rarely discussed and rarely acknowledged. In 2017, Belgian model Hanne Gaby Odiele became the first high-profile person to publicly identify herself as intersex: someone born with genitals or chromosomes that don't easily define a person as male or female.

Odiele was born with androgen insensitivity syndrome. Her DNA was XY, which traditionally leads to male sexual characteristics. But that didn't happen in her case. Her cells didn't respond to the male hormone androgen, as they do in most XY individuals; as she was developing in her mother's womb, she developed testes, but they didn't emerge from inside her body. Instead, she was born with what appeared to be a vulva and a vagina. But she didn't have a uterus.

At the age of 10, she was told she couldn't have children and had her testes removed because her parents were told that if she didn't have the surgery, she might get cancer. But, Odiele said, the statistics don't bear that out: The risk of cancer is no greater for intersex people than it is for anyone else.

"I think the surgeries are done mostly out of fear of nonbinary bodies," she said.

But those surgeries themselves can lead to complications: Odiele mentioned a 13-year-old intersex girl who developed osteoporosis after having surgery. Besides, the operations are irreversible, and they're often performed without the patient's consent, at the direction of parents or doctors.

An estimated 1.7 percent of children are born intersex, but it's seldom discussed. In fact, it's so rarely talked about that Odiele's parents didn't know about her condition. They were, as she said, "half-informed," and were counseled not to tell anyone about her identity.

"They never heard the word, they never heard the term, they never heard even my condition until I found it."

Odiele herself felt alone. "I always felt like I was the only one like me," she said in an interview with The Guardian, "that I had this weird thing going on — having to go and see the doctor for my genitals, thinking, 'What the hell is wrong with me?'"

Understanding dawned when she came across a story in a Dutch teen magazine about an intersex woman who couldn't have children. When she saw the story, it was like a lightbulb went on, and she realized the magazine was describing her, too. She confronted her doctor, who told her, "Yes, you're right,

you finally found out."

The doctor had known all along and hadn't said anything. Odiele knew something was different about her, though.

"I always felt very sheltered. I knew something was wrong, but I didn't really know what. They were (sic) always told me, 'It's all fine, just it's all good. Complete normal girl. I knew stuff was different. Like why would I would go to the doctor and have to take my pants off, every single time? It makes you feel a little bit — feel ashamed."

Even after Odiele discovered the truth, her doctor told her to keep it to herself, warning her that "no one will understand you, you will never find anybody to love you, like this whole thing. ... but after a few years, it starts to wear on you, and you want to tell it."

So she did.

She confided in a group of friends and found that her doctor's fears were unfounded. Not only was she accepted, she also found love.

"My husband was one of the first ones in my friend group that knew. It was very easy to tell him; somehow, we were already longtime friends. Then I had a lovely group of friends that I told like shortly after, and it was never really a problem for anyone."

She also discovered she wasn't the only one, after all.

"Once I knew what it was, and that I was not alone, for me it was a new beginning," she said.

"It helped my confidence, knowing I wasn't the only one anymore," she said. On the other hand, she also become more comfortable with expressing herself as an individual: "I didn't have to follow the norm, because I wasn't the norm. I think that was good."

Her discovery and acceptance of who she was encouraged her to pursue modeling, which she described as "the most female job in the world." Traveling to Paris for a Vogue photo shoot and, later, to the United States, she admits she felt like she was "playing the system a little bit."

The only thing really holding her back was that she, in her own words, had "two left feet" and "walked alike a boy." But that changed after an accident that nearly took her life at age 18. She was crossing the street when she was hit by a car that had run a red light. The accident broke her arms and legs, and left her with bleeding on the brain.

She recovered, but had to undergo rehab in order to walk again. It gave her a reason to practice her walk — and reinvent it. With work, she not only was able to walk again, she was able to walk like a model.

She met her husband shortly after that, and became an advocate for intersex individuals, speaking out against the practice of performing surgery without consent and in favor of acceptance for those like her.

In embracing her identity as intersex, she realized it wasn't her entire identity — far from it.

"Intersex doesn't have to be who you are," she said. "It can just be a small part of your identity. It's not the end of the world. It's quite special once you get into it and accept it."

"It's kind of magical, right?"

— Hanne Gaby Odiele

Marcie Free
Worlds Collide

Mark Free found success singing lead vocals for the melodic metal band King Kobra in the 1980s.

King Kobra was formed by drummer Carmine Appice, who had just finished a two-year stint with Ozzy Osbourne's band, having already played with the likes of Paul Stanley (KISS), Ted Nugent and, early in his career, with the psychedelic proto-metal band Vanilla Fudge.

Appice stood out in King Kobra as the only guy with dark hair. The other four members all had long, blond locks. It was 1983, and that look was starting to define the hair metal genre. Bands like Poison, Warrant and Twisted Sister not only grew their hair long, but they spandex pants and eye makeup that made them look almost (but not quite) like women.

Androgyny in rock dated back to David Bowie and the New York Dolls, if not earlier, but hair metal bands took it to a new level. They not only looked androgynous, they straddled the fence with names like Pretty Boy Floyd, Britny Fox, Girlschool, and the aforementioned Twisted Sister.

Oddly, though, they played metal. Granted, it was a more melodic, hook-laden style, but it was still some of the loudest, most aggressive and bombastic music out there. And behind the makeup, band members like Dee Snider — the most glammed out Sister of all — weren't the kind to take any B.S. When an Australian politician used Twisted Sister's hit We're Not Gonna Take It in an ad without Snider's permission, he not only took legal action, he challenged the guy to a fight.

In this paradoxical world of tough guys who dressed almost like drag queens, Free and King Kobra fit right in. Apart from Appice, their look was typical hairspray-and-eyeliner, but their music was heavy. "Original wailer Mark Free, captured in full-throttle sex sneer... embodied the genre's latent angrogyny...," Kenneth Herzog wrote in a review on allmusic.com.

King Kobra gained exposure in 1986 with Iron Eagle (Never Say Die), the title track to the movie of the same name — a movie in the vein of Top Gun, but far less successful.

On tour, the band opened for the likes of KISS and Iron Maiden, and Free was at the forefront. Free's voice has been compared to that of Steve Perry. But like Judas Priest frontman Rob Halford, who hid the fact that he was gay for years, Free kept her true identity hidden for decades.

Even after having a sex change and becoming Marcie Free in 1993, she didn't feel comfortable with being a transsexual "poster child."

Free formed the band Unruly Child in 1992 but left the music business three years later, moving to Michigan (where "it was easier to blend in") and dropping out of the public eye.

"...I am transsexual and the world was not ready for the likes of me or anyone like me," Free said in an interview with melodicrock.com. "After I announced that I could no longer live as Mark my whole musical world quickly fell apart."

Free said she was deeply hurt when people who had been her friends shunned her after she came out. People she'd worked with in the past suddenly wanted nothing to do with her: "It was like I had the plague or something."

Appice said he learned of Free's sex change from fellow rocker Eddie Money, who said Free had auditioned for a friend's band. His reaction, according to Appice: "Pretty f---ed up or what?"

Appice didn't believe it until he met Free for lunch.

When Appice got King Kobra back together in 2010, Free wasn't invited. He blamed a dispute over Appice's desire to release a DVD that captured one of the band's old live gigs — and on the fact that Free "wanted to play wimpier music." Despite Free's sex change, Appice continued to call her "Mark."

Faced with reactions like that, Free fell back into a pattern of substance abuse, using drugs and alcohol in an effort to cope that only made things worse. "I seriously thought I would never sing again," she said in 2010.

But she found faith in God, got sober and realized she missed singing. In 2010, she reunited with Unruly Child for a new album called *Worlds Collide*. Other releases followed in 2014, 2017 and 2019. Not only is she singing and recording again, but Free's experience has become far more positive.

Her second stint with Unruly Child has brought her the kind of acceptance she was denied after she first came out.

She told Rockpit in 2017: "It's like working with your family, everyone is so close."

"Life is to learn as much as you can, educate yourself and to be at one with nature."

— Marcie Free

50 UNDEFEATED

Katherine Johnson
It All Adds Up

Katherine Johnson didn't just help break down the color barrier, she was instrumental in ensuring the success of America's space program.

She was one of three black students — and the only woman — selected as the first African-Americans to attend graduate school at West Virginia University in 1939, but success was nothing new to her even then. She'd been promoted several grades in school, began high school at the age of 10, and started attending classes at historically black West Virginia State College at the age of 13.

She didn't stay at West Virginia University, but left to start a family with her husband and, later, became a teacher (a career she'd started before accepting the admission to grad school). In 1952, however, she found a new opportunity: The all-black West Area Computing Section at the National Advisory Committee for Aeronautics' (NACA) Langley Laboratory was hiring, and it was headed by Dorothy Vaughn, a fellow West Virginian.

Johnson and her husband moved to Newport News, and she began working at Langley in a position that involved analyzing data from test flights and investigating a plane crash that had been caused by wake turbulence.

When the U.S. entered the space race following the Soviet Union's launch of its Sputnik satellite, NACA was renamed NASA, and Johnson came with the package. Using her expertise in mathematics, she calculated the flight trajectory for Alan Shepherd's inaugural manned mission to space aboard Freedom 7, and co-authored a report setting forth equations on orbital space flight. (In doing so, she became the first woman in the Flight Research Division to receive an author's credit on a research report.)

When John Glenn was set to lead an orbital mission aboard Freedom 7 in 1962, he declined to rely on computer computations that were set to guide the capsule from liftoff to splashdown. Instead, he told engineers to "get the girl" — Johnson — to run the numbers by hand and make sure they checked out. "If she says they're good, I'm ready to go."

Johnson received NASA's Apollo Group Achievement Award as well as the agency's Lunar Spacecraft and Operations Group Achievement Award. She also received the Langley Research Center Special Achievement Award five times: in 1971, 1980, 1984, 1985, and 1986 — the year she retired after 33 years at Langley.

She received the Presidential Medal of Freedom, the nation's highest civilian honor, in 2015, and passed away in 2020. Her work was dramatized in the movie *Hidden Figures*, where she was portrayed by Taraji P. Henson, in 2016.

> *"I counted everything. I counted the steps to the road, the steps up to church, the number of dishes and silverware I washed … anything that could be counted, I did."*
>
> — Katherine Johnson

Stephen Jackson
Legacy

The 6-year-old girl sat on the shoulders of former NBA player Stephen Jackson, who held her aloft days after her father, George Floyd, died in police custody.

The officer was charged with murder.

Floyd had been Jackson's close friend, and Jackson now pledged he would walk 6-year-old Gianna down the aisle when the time came.

That's just who he is.

Jackson had overcome plenty on his own. The son of a single mother who worked two jobs, he had endured tragedy before: His half-brother had died from head injuries when Jackson was just 16.

Donald Buckner Jr. had been being jumped by two men and beaten over the head with a lead pipe and bottles. He was still clinging to life when Jackson visited him in intensive care, where he had 17 staples put in his head. His breathing was shallow, and the outlook wasn't good. But Jackson held his brother's hand to reassure him. He promised to take care of him.

He never got the chance.

So he decided to take are of everyone else, instead.

Speaking in a 2012 interview with Ken Robinson for spurs.com, the San Antonio Spurs website, his mother Judy explained how his brother's death transformed Jackson:

"From that point on, he has been a giving person. He would give you the clothes off his back. I've watched him on numerous occasions give to people. There was a homeless man, standing on the side of a street in Atlanta. Stephen stopped and gave him money He loves to give, and he doesn't even think about it."

Jackson grew up in Port Arthur, Texas, which he described as a "hellhole" where buying a gun is "as easy as buying candy." There were "honest, churchgoing people" in Port Arthur, he said, but more than half of those who lived there were "doing the same thing: selling drugs and gang-banging." There was one main street, which consisted of eight low-income housing complexes.

Everyone knew everyone else.

One of the people Jackson knew was George Floyd, who played basketball, too. At 6-foot-6, Floyd was 2 inches shorter than Jackson; other than that minor discrepancy, however, the two looked remarkably similar. Jackson called him his "twin."

Floyd grew up in Houston, less than an hour away from Port Arthur, and Jackson had met him through a mutual friend. One day, the friend told Jackson he was bringing Floyd down from Houston. Jackson remembered their first meeting in an interview with ESPN:

"So he came, and he's like, 'I'm bringing my homeboy Floyd down here next week. He played basketball, too, but y'all look alike. You might have the same dad.' I'm like, please, man. So he brings Floyd down, I look at Floyd, and the first thing we both say is, 'Who's your daddy?' From looking alike and from that day forward, we just had a bond."

"Big Floyd," as he was known, played football and basketball at Yates High School in Houston, where his acrobatic catches helped the football team reach the state 5A championship game. Jackson, meanwhile, was so good at basketball he led Lincoln High School in Port Arthur to the Texas state title as a junior, but academic problems kept him from playing in college. Plans to play at the University of Arizona didn't pan out because his scores on the SAT and ACT were too low. He attended Butler Community College in Kansas for one semester

but didn't play there.

Still, he not only played in the 1996 McDonald's All-American Boys Game — a showcase for the nation's best graduating high school seniors — where he scored 21 points to lead all scorers and pace the East to a 120-105 victory.

Kobe Bryant scored 13 points in that game.

Jackson went on to the NBA, but he had to work to get there. Selected late in the second round of the draft by the Phoenix Suns, he didn't make the team and wound up with the La Crosse Catbirds with the minor Continental Basketball Association.

Over the next four years, he played professionally in Australia, the Dominican Republic and Venezuela, where his scoring average of 22.8 points a game ranked third in the league in 1999, and his 42.6 percent average from beyond the 3-point line was second-best.

The next year, he made his NBA debut with the New Jersey Nets. He played on the Nets' championship team in 2003 and averaged 15.1 points a game over a career that spanned 14 seasons with eight NBA teams.

Throughout his career, he was the kind of player who took care of the people he cared about, just as he'd vowed to take care of his brother. Sometimes, though, it didn't end well. In the 2004-05 season, he served a 30-game suspension for his role in what became known as "Malice at the Palace," a brawl in a game between Jackson's Indiana Pacers and the Detroit Pistons at the Palace in Auburn Hills, Michigan.

Near the end of the game, with the Pacers holding a safe lead, the Pacers' Ron Artest fouled Ben Williams hard as Williams was going to the basket. Williams responded by pushing Artest, and it was on. The players were separated, and Artest took himself out of it by lying down on the scorer's table. That's when someone in the stands threw a beer at Artest, who jumped up and ran into the stands and started swinging. Jackson followed him and began throwing punches, too.

"I'm with these guys more than I'm with my family during the course of the year, so these are like my brothers," he later said. "I was raised to be a protector and to be with my brothers through thick and thin. When he went, I just went with him."

His assessment of the situation? "I regret how we handled it. I don't regret defending my teammate. I don't regret that. I regret going into the stands and punching fans. I regret that totally."

Most of the time, though, Jackson showed his protective instincts in other ways.

A year after that brawl, he spent $500,000 of his own money to build an afterschool center with computers, a basketball court and classrooms in Port Arthur after Hurricane Rita wreaked destruction on the Gulf Coast city.

In 2008, while playing with the Golden State Warriors, he created the Jack 1 Foundation, a nonprofit that bears his nickname, to support programs that would develop and empower youth, regardless of their economic status. That year, he received the team's community service award, as well as the NBA Community Assist Award for the month of August.

Jackson retired from the NBA in 2015, but five years later, he was back in the news following another tragedy: His friend George Floyd had been killed. A police officer in Minneapolis had knelt on his neck for nearly nine minutes as Floyd pleaded for him to stop.

"I can't breathe," he said.

"Mama."

"Please."

"I'm about to die."

Floyd, 46, was nonresponsive for nearly 3 minutes before the officer got up, according to a criminal complaint. One of the officers checked for a pulse but couldn't find one. Floyd was finally taken to the hospital, where later pronounced dead after emergency room after first responders and E.R. staff members spent nearly an hour trying to revive him.

Recalling his friend, Jackson described Floyd as "a gentle giant."

"He was a protector, a provider. He wanted everybody to be happy and have a good time. That was his thing."

He left behind five children, including a 6-year-old daughter named Gianna.

Just four months before Floyd's death, another young girl named Gianna was killed in a helicopter crash with her father: Kobe Bryant, who had played in the McDonald's All-American Boys Game with Stephen Jackson more than two decades earlier. Across the country, memorial services and tributes honored Bryant, who had finished a 20-year career as one of the top 10 players in NBA history. Gianna, his 13-year-old daughter, had been a promising basketball player in her own right.

The deaths of Kobe and Gianna Bryant produced an outpouring of grief and sympathy for a black man and his daughter. But Floyd's death in police custody reminded the nation of how much was still left undone in the fight for equal rights for black Americans.

As they had following Bryant's death, thousands made their feelings known after the death of George Floyd — only this time, they turned out in the streets across the nation to protest police brutality and the twin scourges of racist hate and violence.

Stephen Jackson was among them, appearing with Gianna's mother, Roxie Washington, at a press conference in front of Minneapolis City Hall.

Speaking of Gianna Floyd, he asked, "Why do we have to see her pain? Why do we have to see a daughter get raised without her father?"

As he had for his brother so many years earlier, Jackson pledged that he would be there for the daughter of the man he'd called his twin.

Addressing Gianna's mother, he said: "I'm going to walk her down the aisle, I'm going to be there for her, I'm going to be there to wipe your tears.

"Floyd might not be here, but I'm here for her. I'm here to get justice, and we're going to get justice for my brother. We're not leaving. We're going to keep fighting."

The tragedy is that, sometimes, overcoming prejudice is left to the next generation.

So it is with George Floyd.

Stephen Jackson is adamant: "George Floyd is going to be the name of change," Jackson said.

If you ask Gianna, he already is.

Carried on Jackson's shoulders at that press conference in Minneapolis, she smiled and shouted triumphantly, "Daddy changed the world!"

"Everybody standing side by side, that's the only way it's gonna get done, and I stand for that. We gotta hold everyone accountable now."

— Stephen Jackson

50 UNDEFEATED

Sources

Academy of Achievement staff (1991, June 29). Interview: Susan Butcher champion dog-sled racer. *Achievement.org*.
Akcam, T. (2012). *The young Turks' crime against humanity: The Armenian genocide and ethnic cleansing in the Ottoman Empire.* Princeton University Press.
Alexandria Times staff (2010, May 27). Slavery and freedom, embodied. *Alexandria Times*.
Altimari, D. (2010, March 9). 'Operation Innocence' asks: Will DNA evidence free 700 inmates? *The Hartford Courant*.
Americans United for Separation of Church and State (2012, September 10). Tenn. Teacher sanctioned for supporting atheist student Krystal Myers. *OpposingViews.com*.
Antoine, J. (2012, September 28). Back from the brink of depression. *HuffingtonPost.com*.
Apeles, T. (2006, December 18). A dark history of Canada: Japanese internments. *FinalCall.com*.
Asimus, Bodie (2003, September 22). Yarri: A frontier story. *Australian Broadcasting Corp*.
Associated Press (1968, October 31). Kathy Kusner is first woman jockey. *Spartanburg Herald*.
Associated Press (1990, March 2). Iditarod racers face worst conditions ever. *Moscow-Pullman Daily News*.
Associated Press (2006, September 26). Inmate exonerated by DNA urges youngsters to work hard. *The Hartford Courant*.
Atlanta Black Star staff (2012, June 21). No money for forced sterilization victims in NC. *Atlanta BlackStar*.
Ayres, A.S. (2012, March 13). Dog earns valor award for shielding owner from domestic violence. *Vetstreet.com*.
Backlander, C. (2012, February 5). Female genital mutilation outlawed in Kenya. *OurEastAfrica.com*.

Baker, A. (2010, August 9). Afghan women and the return of the Taliban. *Time Magazine*.

Bates, C. (2010, October 12). The smile that defies the Taliban: Afghan teenager whose mutilated face shocked the world unveils her new image. *Mail Online*.

BBC News staff (2012, May 28). From child bride to multi-millionaire in India. *BBC News*.

Behling, S. Mary Bliss Parsons. *RootsWeb.Ancestry.com*.

Bender, S. (2005, March 15). The Jeanette Rankin story. *LewRockwell.com*.

Blackburn, J. (2012, March 27). BGT's Big Jon: Bullies drove me to brink. *The Sun*.

Bogart, R. (2007, May 17). Wrongly accused man let free after 18 years and gets $5 million. *Yahoo Voices*.

Bonisch, G. and Rapp, T. (2012, May 28). Rapper Najafi on the fatwa: 'Fundamentalists can't take a joke.' *Der Spiegel*.

Brigham, B. (1995). Glenn Burke: A gay 'hero' with feet of clay. *The Diamond Angle*.

Buzinski, J. (2010, November 3). 'Out. The Glenn Burke story' is a must-see Documentary. *Outsports.com*.

Catholic Herald staff (1980, January 18). Why the Soviet regime is attacking Christian critics. *Catholic Herald*.

Cayleff, S., Babe (1996). *The life and legend of Babe Didrikson Zaharias*. University of Illinois Press.

CBC News staff (2010, August 18). Inuit get federal apology for forced relocation. *CBC.ca*.

Cooperman, Alan (2006, July 4). Fallen soldier gets a Bronze Star but no Pagan star. *The Washington Post*.

Corrections (2009, March 26). *The Washington Post*.

Dehghan, S.K. (2012, May 14). Iranian rapper faces death threats and fatwa for 'blasphemous' song. *The Guardian*.

Dorr, G.M. (2008, November 6). Buck v. Bell. *Encyclopedia Virginia*.

Engelhardt, M. (2011, June 15). Living with conviction: The James Tillman story. *Goodwin College News*.

Erdbrink, T. (2012, May 14). Rapper faces death threats in Iran over song. *The New York Times*.

Fitts, R.K. (2008). *Wally Yonamine: The man who changed Japanese baseball*. University of Nebraska Press.

Frankl, V. (2006). *Man's Search for Meaning*. Beacon Press.

Galloway, A. (2009, December 16). The art of remembering. *Seven Days*.

Gerlach, C. (2010). *Extremely violent societies: Mass violence in the twentieth-century world*. Cambridge University Press.

Gill, B. (1982). PCPFL: 1940-45. *The Coffin Corner, Vol. 4, No. 7*.

Gill, B. (1987). Jackie Robinson: Pro football prelude. *The Coffin Corner, Vol. 9, No. 3*.

Gipe, G. (1978). *The Great American Sports Book*. Doubleday.

Goldstein, P. (2012, June 5). Kirk Douglas on the blacklist: Why Hollywood showed so little courage. *Los Angeles Times*.

Grigsby Bates, K. (2010, October 13). Bibi Aisha, disfigured Afghan woman featured on 'Time' cover, visits U.S.

Gutskey, E. (1989, June 18). Warming up to Wally: Yonamine, first American to play in Japan, was not an instant hit. *Los Angeles Times*.

Hardingham-Gill, T. (2010, October 31). 'I considered suicide after being tormented by bullies': Susan Boyle reveals she was emotionally abused by gang. *The Daily Mail*.

Hills, B. (1993, March 13). The last angry Ainu. *BenHills.com*.

Hoose, P. (2009). *Twice Toward Justice*. Farrar, Strauss and Giroux.

Iltis, T. (2010, September 4). Persecution of Roma worsens in Europe. *Green Left*.

"Inspirational Quotes: Katherine Johnson," wearetechwomen.com.

Irons, P. (2003, February 16). Forced sterilization: a stain on California. *Los Angeles Times*.

Jefferies, M. (2009, November 17). Susan Boyle: I was bullied and beaten at school for being slow. *Daily Record*.

Joshua, J. (2011, March 30). 'Natural citizenship' call for blackbirding descendants gathers momentum. *Vanuatu Daily Post*.

Julian, J.W. (1892). *The life of Joshua R. Giddings*. A.C. McClurg.

Kangsen, M. (2003, June 18). Joseph Shabalala. *Singers.com*.

Kitchen Sisters (2008, July 31). Birth of Rice-A-Roni: The Armenian-Italian treat. *NPR.org*.

Knopper, S. (2011, February 18). Ladysmith Black Mambazo finds freedom in song. *Chicago Tribune*.

Kommersant (2012, September 13). Tambov priest fired over Pussy Riot support. *RIA Novosti*.

Kristof, N.D. (2012, February 29). Born to not get bullied. *The New York Times*.

Lakshmi, R. (2008, March 15). With reports of violence, anger ignites beyond Tibet. *The Washington Post*.

Lautenberg, F.R. (2007, May 10). Lautenberg commends Negro Baseball Leagues, Larry Doby. Press release.

Leukhardt, B. and Owens, D. (2009, December 30). DNA evidence that freed James Tillman linked to Virginia prisoner. *The Hartford Courant*.

Lewis, F. (2011, March 2). Celebrated in 2 worlds: Yonamine was the first post-World War II American in Japanese baseball.

http://www.hollywoodreporter.com/live-feed/game-thrones-season-3-poster-390790 *Honolulu Star-Advertiser*.

Lombardo, P.A. (2008). *Three generations, no imbeciles: Eugenics, the Supreme Court, and Buck v. Bell*. JHU Press.

Lusher, A. (2012, May 12). Teacher tells of choosing song that set Jonathan Antoine and Charlotte Jaconelli on road to stardom on Britain's Got Talent. *The Telegraph*.

Maclellan, N. (2012, September 4). South Sea islanders unite in Australia.

Islands Business.

Marcum, D. (2007, May 13). Crowning moment: Roosevelt prom queen a transgender pioneer. *The Fresno Bee.*

McLean, T. (2011, March 22). Vanuatu raps Australia over 'blackbirding.' *The Australian.*

McNamara, E. (2012, October 21). Activists seek pardon for Connecticut witches. *Southington Patch.*

Moore, J.T. (1988). *Pride against prejudice: The biography of Larry Doby.* ABC-CLIO

MSNBC staff (2012, June 20). North Carolina budget drops payment to forced sterilization victims. *MSNBC.com.*

Murashko, A. (2012, February 25). Atheist student's editorial on discrimination at school censored. *The Christian Post.*

Munoz, H. (2010, April 13). Duane Foster pleads guilty in 1988 case. *The Hartford Courant.*

Munro, C. (2011, April 7). Yarri the brave: Australia's forgotten hero. *Community Tracker.*

Norton, Cherry (2000, August 8). Left-handers more 'creative but forgetful.' *The Independent.*

Obare, O. (2011, February 8). Female MPs draft bill to outlaw FGM. *StandardMedia.co.ke.*

Paterson, T. (2012, May 17). 'Blasphemous' rapper Shahin Najafi goes into hiding after Iran's hardline clerics put $100,000 bounty on his head. *The Independent.*

Peterson, R.W. (1997). *Pigskin: The early years of pro football.*

Pierce, J.K. (2006, June 12). Scopes trial. *American History* magazine. Oxford University Press.

Provost, Stephen H. "Mark Twain's Nevada," Dragon Crown Books, 2022.

Rank, A. (2012, February 17). Forgotten hero: Washington broke NFL's color barrier in 1946. *NFL.com.*

Resture, J. (2012, May 14). Easter Island and the blackbirders. *JaneResture.com.*

Ricks, M.K. (1998, August 12). Escape on the Pearl. *The Washington Post.*

Round, S. (2011, September 26). Vanuatu chiefs to visit historic blackbirding sites in Queensland. *Radio New Zealand.*

Sailor, C. (2012, March 30). George Takei finds new success in activism, social media. *The Olympian.*

Seay, A. (2012, August 8). Pieces of Northampton: Witchcraft in the valley. *Paradise City Press.*

Shatterly, Margot Lee. "Katherine Johnson Biography," nasa.gov.

Shay, G. (2009). What we can learn about appeals from Mr. Tillman's case: More lessons from another DNA exoneration. *Western New England University School of Law.*

Sheppard, K. (2012, February 13). 'The Loving story': How an interracial couple changed a nation. *Mother Jones.*

Silverman, S.M. (2012, October 4). Karen Klein, bullied school monitor, now helping other victims. *People.com*.

Simpson, J. (2012, May 26). Jeannette Rankin: How dearly we need you now. *Journal of Peace and Freedom*, freevenice.org.

Snowden, D. (1987, June 10). Ladysmith Black Mambazo: Zulu dream harmonies sung a cappella. *Los Angeles Times*.

Stowe, H.B. (1853). *A key to Uncle Tom's cabin*. Sampson Low, Son & Co.

Takei, G. (2012, April 27. We Japanese Americans must not forget our wartime internment. *The Guardian*.

Temman, M. (2006, May 10). The Ainu will be voiceless in Japan. *Liberacion*.

Thau, L. (2012, October 11). Lhakpa Tsering: Man on fire. *Strangers*, CRW.com

Thomas, D. (2002, June 27). A wise man keeps on singing. *The Telegraph*.

Thurbur, J. (2006, August 7). Susan Butcher, 51, four-time winner of Iditarod inspired global interest in the race. *Los Angeles Times*.

Tsering, L. (2012). *Tibettheatre.org*.

Tzemach Lemmon, G. (2010, November 21). Bibi Aisha's pain isn't over. *The Daily Beast*.

Van Natta, D. (2011, June 25). Babe Didrikson Zaharias's legacy fades. *The New York Times*.

Vernon, J. (2008, spring). Jim Crow, meet Lieutenant Robinson: A 1944 court-martial. *Prologue Magazine, Vol. 40, No. 1*.

Walters, M. (2004, winter). Yarri of Wiradjuri: The story of a Gundagai Aboriginal hero. *The Hummer, Vo. 3, No. 4*.

Wasniewski, M.A. (2006). *Women in Congress, 1917-2006*. Government Printing Office.

Waterhouse, D. (2007, May 15) Fresno High schoolers make transgender history. *Community Alliance*.

Watson, P. (2009, November 29). Inuit were moved 2,000 km in Cold War manoeuvring. *Toronto Star*.

Weber, B. (2011, March 4). Wally Yonamine dies at 85; changed Japanese baseball. *The New York Times*.

Whaley, S. (2006, March 2). Sergeant's space left blank: Fallen Guardsman's Wiccan faith unrecognized. *LasVegas Review-Journal*.

Willett, H.G. (2012, February 23). Lenoir City High School won't publish atheist student's editorial on religion in schools. *Knoxville News Sentinel*.

Winkler, M.M. (2008). *Spartacus: Film and history*. John Wiley & Sons

Witte, D. (2009, May 24). Pakistan intensifies effort with thrust into Swat's main city. *The Washington Post*.

Wolff, A. (2008, October 8). Three pioneers deserved to be in the Pro Football Hall of Fame. *SI.com*.

Yousafzai, M. (2009, January 19). Diary of a Pakistani schoolgirl. *BBC News*.

Zielenziger, M. (1997, October 4). Japan admits it wasn't there first. *The Baltimore Sun*.

Stephen H. Provost

The author writes about American highways, mutant superheroes, mythic archetypes, and pretty much anything he wants. A former journalist, historian, philosopher, and novelist, he lives in Carson City, Nevada. And he loves cats. Read his blogs and keep up with his latest activities at stephenhprovost.com and find his books at dragoncrownbooks.com.

www.ingramcontent.com/pod-product-compliance
Lightning Source LLC
Chambersburg PA
CBHW061252110426
42742CB00012BA/1890